Breaking Through the Barriers of Life

The Power of Perseverance

by
Dr. Joseph M. Ripley, Sr.

Harrison House
Tulsa, Oklahoma

The Power of Perseverance: Breaking Through the Barriers of Life
ISBN 1-57794-353-8
Copyright © 2003 by Dr. Joseph M. Ripley, Sr.
P.O. Box 490346
College Park, GA 30349

Published by Harrison House, Inc.
P.O. Box 35035
Tulsa, OK 74153

Contents

Dedication

To my wife, Marjanita, for her uncompromising commitment to God that always makes me thankful for finding my true Proverbs 31 woman enabling me to obtain the favor of the Lord;

To my children, April, Heather, and Joey, for their encouragement and for their willingness to share Daddy with the world;

And to my church family, The Body of Christ Church International, USA, for being the evidence of *the power of perseverance.*

Introduction

My son, Joey, enjoys running a seemingly endless variety of programs on his personal computer. From simple math programs to sophisticated multitask software, he operates each with relative ease. When asked how he can run such a wide array of programs, he says, "We have a great system capable of running it all."

When you get right down to it, Christians also have a great system capable of running it all. From the healing of minor ailments to resolving complex human dilemmas, the Word of God provides practicable solutions to every aspect of our lives, if we will put it into practice.

In the following pages, we will discuss several elements necessary to living a successful Christian life. What it boils down to in the end, however, is perseverance. We can do everything according to God's Word, but we will still come up short if we do not persevere till the end. May you be encouraged to break through the barriers in your life and persevere till you win.

1

Be an Imitator of God

Endurance and constancy are prolific attributes of God. The things He creates endure. Throughout the Bible, we see that no matter what, when, where, why, or how things happen, God remains forever the same. He wants this to be said of us as well. Ephesians 5:1 AMP (emphasis mine) says,

> Be *imitators* of God [copy Him and follow His example], as well-beloved children [imitate their father].

The King James Version translates the word *imitators* as *followers*. The Greek word from which these terms are translated is where we get our English word *mimic*, which means, to imitate.

Now, certainly, none of us will be hurling new planets into the solar system or launching new galaxies into orbit around the universe. And you have probably noticed that the mountain chains around the earth have remained constant, with the exception of a relatively small number of significant seismic events. I believe the heart of Paul's exhortation speaks more of a decisive inward determination in contrast to moving things to a physical destination. God finishes what He starts. He perseveres until his goal is achieved. In the course of our lives, this constant determination of God enables those who mimic it to endure and subsequently overcome opposition of any kind.

Our English language is sometimes woefully inadequate in rendering expressions that are common in Greek, the language from which the New Testament was translated. The instructions translated *be followers* and *be imitators* in Ephesians 5:1 are rendered in the present imperative tense. That means there is a command to do something in the future, which involves continuous or repeated action. When this expression prohibits an action, it usually carries with it the implication of stopping an action that has been taking place.

To illustrate this point, consider a lawn planted around a house. The lawn consists of grass that is constantly growing. The homeowner is responsible for mowing the lawn; however, one cutting will not stop the grass from growing. Because of this, the grass will have to be cut on a regular basis. As long as grass grows, it will need to be cut.

In our lives, just because we overcome a challenge or obstacle once does not necessarily stop it or others from presenting themselves again. I use this very simple illustration to point out that everyday life requires active, ongoing participation.

We must remain constant in our response to challenges; and although many things in our lives are typical and routine, we must expect the unexpected. We like the predictable, but realistically, one of the only true constants in life is change. In order for us to walk in victory, we must discover that it is not *what* happens to us that is the issue, but rather *how we handle* what happens to us.

Imitate the Godly Response

By imitating Jesus and responding like He did in an ongoing, consistent way, we can walk in the peace of God and live successful Christian lives. Temptations, trials, and tests come with the territory for believers, but we can learn a great deal from studying how Jesus responded to them.

> These things I have spoken unto you, that in me ye might have peace. In the world ye shall have tribulation: but be of good cheer; I have overcome the world.
>
> John 16:33

Seek (aim at and strive after) first of all His kingdom and His righteousness (His way of doing and being right), and then all these things taken together will be given you besides. So do not worry or be anxious about tomorrow, for tomorrow will have worries and anxieties of its own. Sufficient for each day is its own trouble.

Matthew 6:33–34 AMP

In addition to our observation of Jesus, let's consider the following words of encouragement from Paul and James:

No temptation (no trial regarded as enticing to sin), [no matter how it comes or where it leads] has overtaken you and laid hold on you that is not common to man [that is, no temptation or trial has come to you that is beyond human resistance and that is not adjusted and adapted and belonging to human experience, and such as man can bear]. But God is faithful [to His Word and to His compassionate nature], and He [can be trusted] not to let you be tempted and tried and assayed beyond your ability and strength of resistance and power to endure, but with the temptation He will [always] also provide the way out (the means of escape to a landing place), that you may be capable and strong and powerful to bear up under it patiently.

1 Corinthians 10:13 AMP

> Consider it wholly joyful, my brethren, whenever you are enveloped in or encounter trials of any sort or fall into various temptations. Be assured and understand that the trial and proving of your faith bring out endurance and steadfastness and patience.
>
> James 1:2–3 AMP

Upon meditating on these four passages of Scripture, one may conclude that confronting temptations, trials, and tests is akin to taking the football down the field and driving toward the goal. Most of the time, the team that is the most prepared and most determined will win; however, there is one other element that is essential to clench the victory: perseverance. You can be prepared and determined and still not cross the goal line. You could quit just short of the goal, which many are tempted to do when the going gets tough. But don't give up! You must persevere until the victory has been won!

Thank God that He prepares us through His Word and encourages us to possess a winning attitude. In Him we are all viewed as winners and champions. When you learn to see yourself as God sees you and you act accordingly, you will begin to live in victory. You might ask, "How can I walk in that kind of confidence?" The answer is in the Word of God:

> This is the confidence (the assurance, the privilege of boldness) which we have in Him: [we are sure] that if we ask anything (make any request) according to His will (in agreement with His own plan), He listens to and hears us. And if (since) we [positively] know that He listens to us in whatever we ask, we also know [with settled and absolute knowledge] that we have [granted us as our present possessions] the requests made of Him.
>
> 1 John 5:14–15 AMP

I have learned through the Word of God and personal experience that running away from problems is never the solution. In fact, running away may further compound them. As long as problems are permitted to remain in an environment free of spiritual resistance and faith in God's Word, they will remain and continually agitate. It is important to remember that the ultimate goal of all evil spiritual forces is to destroy our faith in God and ultimately eliminate us as viable threats to the kingdom of darkness.

I implore you not to let that happen! God has a part to play and He will do it, but we also have a part to play. Our part is to imitate His ways as revealed in His Word and to persevere to the end as He does. It is then that we will experience victory and enjoy the fruit of our labors.

2

Everything Works Correctly
in the Right Environment

God created people with the ability to function in two environments: the natural and the supernatural. Man is created in God's image; he is a spirit like God is a Spirit. God also fashioned a physical body for man in which his spirit and his soul reside. To put it another way, man is a spirit, he has a soul, and he lives in a body. These components give man access to both the supernatural (or spiritual) environment as well as to the natural (or physical) environment. It is important that perseverance play a large role in both of these environments because there are resistant forces in each.

Environment is defined as the circumstances or conditions surrounding one; the complex of social and cultural conditions affecting the nature of an individual or community.[1] Likewise, the environment for success is a complex of conditions laid out in the Word of God. Throughout this chapter we will examine many of these conditions.

Some people are of the opinion that we are products of our environment. While there is truth to that statement, we also have the power to change our environment. Many times all it takes is a single but resolute decision. A good example of this is a child and his attitude. If the child chooses to have a positive attitude, he creates an amicable and pleasant environment in which to live, work, and play. Of course there are many other factors that can affect our environment— some positive, some negative—but the thing that should impact our lives to the greatest degree is God and His goodness.

In the Book of Genesis, we discover that God created the environment for man, not the man for the environment. Consider this based on the original five-fold purpose of man described in Genesis 1:28, which incidentally, God has never rescinded: "God blessed them, and God said unto them, Be fruitful, and multiply, and replenish the earth, and subdue it: and have dominion." Have you ever noticed that God does not give orders to people who cannot carry them out? The Lord has created an environment in which everything He instructs man to do can be fulfilled. This arrangement is not only pleasing to God, but it is most beneficial to man.

All the Tools We Need

God did not just place us in the earth and then leave us to fend for ourselves. He has provided all the tools we need to be blessed in this life. And these tools are effective—they come with a lifetime guarantee, because they are based on the eternal promises in God's Word.

God has a wonderful plan and purpose for every person—including you. It is vitally important that you realize this and know that God loves you very much. Everything God does He does on purpose, and there is a clear pattern in the Word of God showing that He uses people to accomplish His will.

The following terms describe a few of the tools available to us so that God can fulfill His purposes through us. Notice that each of these is a character trait that we can develop as we mature in our walks with the Lord.

> *Perseverance:* the action of persisting in or remaining constant to a purpose, idea, or task in the face of discouragement or opposition.

Diligence: perseverance in carrying out action and nothing less.

Persistence: the act of holding steadfastly and firmly to a purpose, state, or undertaking despite obstacles, warnings, or setbacks. To refuse to give up or let go; to carry on through despite hardships; to bear with tolerance.

Steadfastness: staying fixed or unchanged; being firmly loyal or constant.

Endurance: the ability to bear trials, have fortitude, perseverance, abide.[2]

Each of these traits has the potential to put us over the top and cause us to succeed in our God-given goals.

Tools with a Lifetime Guarantee

In addition to developing the character traits, which are tools in our spiritual toolbox, God has revealed additional tools in His Word.

This is the love of God, that we keep his commandments: and his commandments are not grievous. For whatsoever is born of God overcometh the world: and this is the victory that overcometh the world, even our faith.

1 John 5:3

Note the awesome potential inherent in every born-again child of God to overcome the world. Faith is one of our God-given tools by which we attain victory. In the face of all temptations, tests, and trials that come our way, we are more than conquerors through Christ who strengthens us. (See Rom. 8:37 and Phil. 4:13.) Further, we are informed in 2 Peter 1:3–4,

> According as his divine power hath given unto us all things that pertain unto life and godliness, through the knowledge of him that hath called us to glory and virtue: Whereby are given unto us exceeding great and precious promises: that by these ye might be partakers of the divine nature, having escaped the corruption that is in the world through lust.

The Bible reveals that God has given us everything that we will ever need to successfully live our lives. The specific tools that are revealed in this verse are the knowledge of God and the promises of God. These promises are indeed great and precious because they enable us to persevere to victory and claim what is rightfully ours as children of God. He has given us everything we need—everything except an excuse that is.

It is important to note that you can have all the right tools, but that alone is not enough to ensure success. In order for these tools to perform to their capacity, we must create the proper environment for them. Using the right tools in the right environment is key. Next we will explore more ways that we can create the right conditions for an environment of success.

Meditating on God's Word Improves Attitude

Every person born upon the face of the earth has faced resistance and obstacles in life. Some persevere to victory while others succumb to defeat. What is the difference between the victors and the victims? The answer is not so much in what happens to a person, but rather how a person handles what happens to him. One's attitude makes all the difference, and meditating on God's Word is one way to develop a positive, overcoming attitude—an attitude of success.

One of the most fascinating revelations I have received in the Scriptures is that God has already established victory for us before confrontations occur. Take note of the following remarkable statement in the Bible that was spoken by God:

> This book of the law shall not depart out thy mouth; but thou shalt meditate therein day and night, that thou mayest observe to do according

to all that is written therein: for then thou shalt make thy way prosperous, and then thou shalt have good success.

Joshua 1:8

God certainly knows that most Christians will not be found with their heads buried in the Bible twenty-four/seven; however, to those who meditate in the Word on a daily, consistent basis, these promises will be fully realized. This is not a fanatical approach as some might think. The very fact that we are creatures of habit implies that daily study of the Bible may be easily assimilated into our lifestyles. There are so many things we do almost robotically as part of our daily routine, yet we readily add things to our agendas all the time. All it takes is a simple decision. Why not let that something be a commitment to meditate on God's Word every day? Doing so will help develop a winning attitude, which is another of the conditions needed to create the right environment for faith to flourish.

The Amplified Bible renders the last phrase of verse 8 as follows: "Then you shall make your way prosperous, and then you shall deal wisely and have good success." Consider the enormity of this promise. Is it not worth availing ourselves to

God's Word to assure continued success in the affairs of life?

A Fear-Free Environment

Let us get back to our study of the text in Joshua 1, which reveals another factor that will contribute to our success. First, notice the verse that precedes our text, verse 7. We must obey it before proceeding to verse 8:

> Only be thou strong and very courageous, that thou mayest observe to do according to all the law, which Moses my servant commanded thee: turn not from it to the right hand or to the left, that thou mayest prosper withersoever thou goest.

Essentially, one must determine to be strong and courageous. The use of the word *only* indicates that the decision to be strong and courageous must exclude anything that would weaken, hinder, or corrupt such a posture. This implies working in an environment free from fear. It is important to note that the world's system—or the environment of this world—is full of fear and continually poses resistance to all that is of God.

To counteract that fear, we must be strong and courageous. We must enforce our authority as believers in the realm of the spirit to bring that which is of God to bear on the circumstances of life. Breaking through the barriers of life is indeed a spiritual matter. The enforcement of spiritual law is accomplished by applying the Word of God to every situation.

Consider what Jesus said in Matthew 11:12: From the days of John the Baptist until now the kingdom of heaven suffereth violence, and the violent take it by force." The Amplified translation conveys this verse as follows:

> From the days of John the Baptist until the present time, the kingdom of heaven has endured violent assault, and violent men seize it by force [as a precious prize—a share in the heavenly kingdom is sought with most ardent zeal and intense exertion].

We must understand that all of these wonderful blessings and promises of God are not simply going to fall into our laps as ripe cherries from a tree. We must with very enthusiastic zeal through God's Word lay claim to all that is ours in Him. The enemy will attempt to hijack and take hostage anything we confess and possess. We may now understand more clearly why being strong and of good courage precede verse 8 in Joshua 1.

Stay Focused

The spiritual environment in the earth prior to the fall of man was such that it yielded itself to the exercising of faith. When Adam through sin and transgression permitted the earthly environment to be polluted by sin and death, nothing has ever been the same. To this day we must exert faith to counter the curse from the Fall. The good news is that we have been redeemed from the curse of the law, although this does not include all the curse from the Fall. On the other hand, there is a place in God to which believers may strive that may abate the pressure resulting from the curse of the Fall.

Casual observation reveals that few believers are willing to pay the price to strive to that level of spiritual living. I believe the apostle Paul succinctly described such an effort in Philippians 3:12:

> Not as though I had already attained, either were already perfect: but I follow after, if that I may apprehend that for which also I am apprehended of Christ Jesus.

In other words Paul is saying, "I am going after God to discover that for which He is coming after me."

Notice also verses 13–14:

Brethren, I count not myself to have appre-
hended: but this one thing I do, forgetting those
things which are behind, and reaching forth unto
those things which are before, I press toward the
mark for the prize of the high calling of God in
Christ Jesus.

Notice how focused Paul was while pursuing
his goal. Some modern-day Christians are quite
distracted from that kind of focus and may never
realize the fullness of much that God has made
available. Focus is a critical factor to breaking
through life's barriers.

With this in mind, we will look back to our
subject text and note about Joshua 1:7, an admo-
nition to avoid being distracted from the Word of
God, which could in turn precipitate a missed
kingdom opportunity. "Turn not from it to the
right hand or to the left, that thou mayest prosper
whithersoever thou goest." To put it another way,
stick with the Scripture. The Word of God should
be the principle upon which we live our lives and
the absolute rule of our conduct. When we make
the quality decision to live, move, and have our
being according to God's Word, we may be
assured that our course to success is true. (See Acts
17:28.) The Bible is an unchanging standard by
which all things are measured.

To illustrate, one may draw what appears to be a straight line on paper. To the untrained eye, the line may appear perfectly straight. However, if a ruler were placed parallel to the drawn line, any deviation from a truly straight line would become apparent. The practical truth in this illustration is that if the line is shown to be untrue by the ruler, then the necessary correction should be made. As Christians we are encouraged to look to our living standard, the Lord Jesus Christ, and adjust ourselves accordingly.

The Mouth—The Launch pad of Faith

Looking again at Joshua 1:8, God provided specific instructions that when followed, manifest good results. I believe it is a vital element to personalize the Word of God in our lives. When approaching verse 8, we are instructed not to let the Word of God depart out of our *mouths*. It is essential that we not trivialize any portion of God's instructions. Each facet reveals a critical factor that may mean the difference between success and failure as it relates to our part.

The mouth plays a major role in creating the right atmosphere for faith to work. You could say that the mouth is the launch pad of faith. Faith is a matter of the heart, yet for it to work in our lives, it must be verbally expressed. Jesus revealed how faith works when He said,

> Verily I say unto you, That whosoever shall *say* unto this mountain, Be thou removed, and be thou cast into the sea; and shall not doubt in his heart, but shall believe that those things which he *saith* shall come to pass; he shall have whatsoever he *saith*.
>
> Mark 11:23 (emphasis mine)

This truth should come as no surprise since God Himself created the world by His spoken Word. Being made in His image and after His likeness, we basically "create" our "worlds" the same way.

At this point you might ask, "What does all of this have to do with perseverance?" We must persevere to see that our mouths do not speak our own undoing. Amazingly, the Bible has much to say about the use of our mouths and more specifically our tongues. Proverbs 18:21 declares that, "Death and life are in the power of the tongue." Notice it is not death *or* life, but death *and* life. It is imperative that we rule our tongues. If you fill your heart with the Word of God, your mouth will dispense the same. Jesus said, "Out of the abundance of the heart the mouth speaketh" (Matt. 12:34). What we so vitally need is God's Word in our hearts and mouths continually.

Back to our text in Joshua 1, the next specific instruction amplifies the one that precedes it. God said, "Thou shalt meditate therein day and night, that thou mayest observe to do according to all that is written therein." Meditation is not a passive form of study, nor is it deep thought as used in the context of this verse. The Hebrew word translated *meditate* means "to mutter or murmur to oneself," to say repeatedly what the Word of God says.

Pure Lips and Pure Motives

It seems that words are the point of success for the forces of good as well as evil. Looking back at Proverbs 18:21, we see that the words we speak may potentially license spiritual forces of good or evil to gain expression and ultimately manifest themselves in our lives. It is literally a life and death matter. Consider this question from the psalmist:

> What man is he that desireth life, and loveth many days, that he may see good? Keep thy tongue from evil, and thy lips from speaking guile. Depart from evil, and do good; seek peace, and pursue it.
>
> Psalm 34:12–14

Simply defined, *guile* means deceit and dishonesty. If we desire to live long lives full of God's goodness, our tongues must refrain from speaking guile and speak Truth instead.

All of the promises of God are conditional, however. They operate on a simple transaction of cause and effect. Speaking the truth of God's Word is indeed part of the cause, but it is not a mere mechanical stimulus. Rather it is to spring out of pure heart instead of one filled with deceit and dishonesty. God's Word is full of precious promises, but it is also a sword that exposes the motives and intents of our hearts.

> The Word that God speaks is alive and full of power [making it active, operative, energizing, and effective]; it is sharper than any two-edged sword, penetrating to the dividing line of the breath of life (soul) and [the immortal] spirit, and of joints and morrow [of the deepest parts of our nature], exposing and sifting and analyzing and judging the very thoughts and purposes of the heart.
>
> Hebrews 4:12 AMP

So what do we do if our hearts and motives are less than pure? We certainly shouldn't get under condemnation about it, but rather we should be thankful that the situation has been exposed, so we can repent and have our pure hearts restored.

In addition, this passage from Hebrews underscores again that the Word of God is alive and full of power. It is effective. Every single one of the awesome promises of God *will* come to pass when the right conditions are met to create an environment of faith. As we have mentioned, studying, meditating on, and speaking God's Word are all integral conditions that contribute toward creating and maintaining this environment of faith.

Stick with the Instructions

In the pilot series of our *Living in Victory* television broadcast, a "God idea" came to me to use a boxed cake mix to illustrate the importance of following instructions to obtain victory. The back of the box listed all of the ingredients to be added and in what order. Of equal importance were the temperature and the amount of time the batter needed to cook in that environment to obtain a successful result. In a phrase, that cake box preached.

The image of the cake on the front of that box looked good enough to eat, but there was nothing in the box except dry powder. If I wanted what I saw on the box, I had to follow the instructions. Similarly, to some the Bible appears to be just another book full of "dry" words. But God's Word is alive and when it is mixed with other ingredients, placed in the proper environment, and duly acted upon, the result is success.

Some of these essential ingredients include regular church attendance, study and meditation of God's Word, prayer, praise and worship, and fellowship with those of like precious faith. Some believers seem to think that they will get the desired results if they only contribute one or two ingredients to the mix. But just praying all the time, for example, is not enough to create a successful outcome.

Similarly, most realize that the best environment in which to bake a cake is a properly heated oven; however, if we just pour the dry mix into a pan and put it into the oven, there will be no cake. There will be a hot pan with hot powder, but no cake. There are other instructions that must be followed for the cake to turn out right. Likewise, church is a great environment for a believer to thrive in, but all of the other ingredients must be added and the directions followed in order to produce the desired results.

By studying God's Word, we can know all of the instructions God has given us. Then we must put them into practice. When we do, blessing will result. James 1:25 NASB puts it this way:

> But one who looks intently at the perfect law, the law of liberty, and abides by it, not having become a forgetful hearer but an effectual doer, this man will be blessed in what he does.

These things are so basic, but it is easy to let them slide. Our Father knows this, so He included a reminder in His Word: "We ought to give the more earnest heed to the things which we have heard, lest at any time we should let them slip" (Hebrews 2:1). There is an interesting acronym that can be drawn from the word *slip:* Slothful, Lazy, Inactive, and Passive. These elements, if given place, would certainly ensure failure. It is best to read God's instructions and stick with them.

Diligently Maintain Your Spiritual Walk

Perseverance can be likened to a powerful engine. There are a number of things an engine needs to accomplish real work. Talk of automobile engine displacement and horsepower was all the rage during my teen and college years; however, there was little said of lubricants (motor oil, transmission fluids, etc.), fuel octane ratings, tire pressure, and their impact on the overall performance of the vehicle. We dreamed of all the brand-name accessories that could be added to enhance the vehicle, but gave no thought to the necessities of upkeep and maintenance.

The fact is, the most handsome looking car will not perform well if the engine is not tuned, lubricated properly, and timed appropriately. Things that are not visible but are beneath the surface of the glamour substantially impact performance. This principle is true in our lives as well. It is good when we as believers looks the part, but even more important is what goes on "under the hood." What thought is given to daily Bible reading and other disciplines that enhance the believer's "performance"?

Why do some people upon hearing the Gospel move on what they hear and get results, while others hearing the same Gospel attain next to nothing? It often boils down to what is going on beneath the surface in the heart of the person. Diligence to maintain one's spiritual vitality and growth is a key factor for successful Christian living.

Faith Requires Action

One of my pastime pleasures is cooking, especially Crock-Pot slow cooking. I carefully read a recipe and make a list of all the needed ingredients. I then purchase the ingredients from a local grocery store and place them on the kitchen counter. What would happen if I had all of the right ingredients, the Crock-Pot, and the recipe but took no action? Absolutely nothing!

This is the case in some believers' lives. They have a Bible and in some cases, more than one. They attend church and hear the message of the Gospel preached, yet they have little, if any, tractable results. Consider the following passages of Scripture:

> Unto us was the gospel preached, as well as unto them: but the word preached did not profit them, not being mixed with faith in them that heard it.
>
> Hebrews 4:2

> Without faith it is impossible to please and be satisfactory to Him. For whoever would come near to God must [necessarily] believe that God exists and that He is the rewarder of those who earnestly and diligently seek Him [out].
>
> Hebrews 11:6 AMP

Some people have a "one *or* the other" frame of mind concerning what redemption includes, when the Word of God reveals a "one *and* the other" plan. It is commonly understood that forgiveness of sins is part of our redemption; however, many do not realize that in addition to bearing our sins, Jesus also bore our sicknesses. The plan of redemption includes both salvation *and* healing. In Christ we don't have to settle for one or the other. We are forgiven and, as 1 Peter 2:24 reveals, we are also healed by the stripes of Jesus. You might say we can have our cake and eat it too!

I love the idiom my wife uses to describe this issue. She calls it "stopping in Charlotte." The phrase is in reference to someone saying that he will drive from Atlanta, Georgia, to New York City, but the individual stops in Charlotte, North Carolina, *thinking* they have arrived at New York City. In other words the person hasn't gone all the way and he is not in New York City, whether he realizes it or not. He then wonders why he doesn't see the statue of Liberty. What we're saying here is that when some people get saved, they think they've gone all the way; that they've received all God has for them. But in reality there is much more. We can be forgiven *and* we can be healed.

There are definite action steps that must be taken regarding the Word of God upon which we base our quests for success. It is important that we not become our own worst enemies in respect to pursuing our goals. God has a right to expect our participation in the fulfillment of His purpose for our lives.

Referring back to our text in Joshua 1, God provided Joshua (and us through this passage) a sure and effective plan by which He would lead the children of Israel into the land of promise. Joshua's part was to *act as if what God said was true.* Notice also that the solution God provided has an ongoing relevance. It is just as right for us today as it was for Joshua and the children of Israel when God gave the initial instruction. Many things devised by men provide limited remedies, but there is no shelf life, term, or expiration date on the Bible. God told Joshua that as long as he meditated in His Word on an ongoing basis, he would make his way prosperous on an ongoing basis. The same is true for us today.

The challenge with some believers is that they allow their inspiration to evaporate. I recall an advertisement by a leading producer of grape jelly that illustrated a system by which the cooking process "captured" the rising aroma and cycled it back into the batch of jelly to ensure rich flavor. Similarly, that is what meditating on the Word of God will do.

How many times have you been in an absolutely spiritually charged meeting that "spiked" you with inspiration? You know how important it is to go back over the Scripture references as well as your notes to reinforce what you "caught" in your spirit. It is vitally important to reinforce through study and meditation those things you receive. Audio and video recordings are excellent for bringing you back to the inspiring moment, but they are not necessarily a substitute for personal study and meditation in the Word of God. Again we see the principle: it's not just one *or* the other, but one *and* the other. We need to be fed spiritually by those called of God, but we also need to meditate on and study God's Word for ourselves.

3

More Keys to Success

First Kings 3:5–15 tells about the keys King
Solomon discovered that brought him success.

In Gibeon the Lord appeared to Solomon in a
dream by night: and God said, Ask what I shall give
thee. And Solomon said, Thou hast showed unto
thy servant David my father great mercy, according
as he walked before thee in truth, and in righteousness, and in uprightness of heart with thee; and
thou hast kept for him this great kindness, that
thou hast given him a son to sit on his throne, as it
is this day. And now, O Lord my God, thou hast
made thy servant king instead of David my father:
and I am but a little child: I know not how to go
out or come in. And thy servant is in the midst of
thy people which thou hast chosen, a great people,
that cannot be numbered nor counted for multi-
tude. Give therefore thy servant an understanding
heart to judge thy people, that I may discern
between good and bad: for who is able to judge this
thy so great a people? And the speech pleased the
Lord, that Solomon had asked this thing. And God

said unto him, Because thou hast asked this thing, and hast not asked for thyself long life; neither hast asked riches for thyself, nor hast asked the life of thine enemies; but hast asked for thyself understanding to discern judgment; Behold, I have done according to thy words: lo, I have given thee a wise and an understanding heart; so that there was none like thee before thee, neither after thee shall any arise like unto thee. And I have also given thee that which thou hast not asked, both riches, and honour: so that there shall not be any among the kings like unto thee all thy days. And if thou wilt walk in my ways, to keep my statutes and my commandments, as thy father David did walk, then I will lengthen thy days. And Solomon awoke; and, behold, it was a dream. And he came to Jerusalem, and stood before the ark of the covenant of the Lord, and offered up burnt offerings, and offered peace offerings, and made a feast to all his servants.

In the first verses of this text are found some very powerful keys to our covenant of victory with God. It is interesting to note that Solomon's love for God was expressed in his openly active worship of God, his obedience to God's Word, and his liberality in giving. Evidently his expressions of love warranted a response from the Lord. Think of what an amazing thing it was for the Lord to respond personally to Solomon by appearing in his dream and giving him divine assurance that his petition would be granted.

Solomon had the awesome task of governing the children of Israel. And even more challenging was that he was following in his father David's footsteps. In verse 6, we see that Solomon sought God, which is the most basic principle to overcoming any of life's challenges. It is important to remember that no challenge poses a threat that God cannot handle. The key is to exercise our right and privilege to approach God for help.

No doubt there are keys to each of the things that Solomon did *not* ask of the Lord, but it is clear that he received the "master" key to all of life's challenges—wisdom. In addition to wisdom, it is also clearly stated by God that the measure of effectiveness of our lives is in direct relationship to our *willingness* to walk in God's ways.

Some Words of Encouragement

In my pastoral experience, no remark from a counselee was more ridiculous than, "The Bible can't change this mess I'm in." My interpretation of such a remark: "I'm not willing to pay the price to apply the Word of God until victory comes." Stubbornness is the core of ignorance. Perhaps this is a good time to mention some key passages of Scripture by which we can encourage our hearts. Notice how in each of them God's involvement is up close and personal. He wants to help!

> There hath no temptation taken you but such as is common to man: but God is faithful, who will not suffer you to be tempted above that ye are able; but will with the temptation also make a way to escape, that ye may be able to bear it.
>
> 1 Corinthians 10:13

> Without faith it is impossible to please him: for he that cometh to God must believe that He is, and that He is a rewarder of them that diligently seek Him.
>
> Hebrews 11:6

Notice that the *diligent seeker* is promised a reward. As we mentioned at the beginning of the last chapter, *diligence* is "perseverance in carrying out action and nothing less." Effort and initiative are required prerequisites to obtaining victory over life's challenges.

Possess the Mind of Christ

Challenges come with the territory in the life of a believer. In John 16:33, Jesus stated, "These things

I have spoken unto you, that in me ye might have peace. In the world ye shall have tribulation: but be of good cheer; I have overcome the world." There is a phrase commonly used in memorial services to encourage the family and friends of a loved one who has passed on: "Earth has no sorrow that heaven cannot heal." Jesus encouraged us through this verse that He has already overcome the worst the world may hurl our way. When we recognize that Christ is in us, which is the hope of glory, and the fact that we are more than conquerors through Him that loved us, we may confidently move forward to break through the barriers of life. (See Col. 1:27 and Rom. 8:37.)

Philippians 2:5 says, "Let this mind be in you, which was also in Christ Jesus." We need to learn to think as Christ thinks. Can you imagine Jesus thinking in terms of being overcome or defeated by anything? Now, can you imagine letting the mind of Christ think through you? Think of the possibilities that would be open to you.

Now, consider what the Bible says in 1 Corinthians 2:16: "Who hath known the mind of the Lord, that he may instruct him? But we have the mind of Christ." Access to the mind of the Lord is made possible through the Holy Spirit. Jesus said in John 16:13–14,

> When he, the Spirit of truth, is come, he will guide you into all truth: for he shall not speak of himself; but whatsoever he shall hear, that shall he speak: and he will show you things to come. He shall glorify me: for he shall receive of mine, and shall show it unto you.

This is the direct testimony of Jesus revealing the access we have to the mind of Christ.

Ignorance is the breeding ground for fear, and it is a potentially dangerous condition. Consider the word of the Lord from the mouth of the prophet Hosea: "My people are destroyed for lack of knowledge" (Hos. 4:6). Thank God for the Holy Spirit who has been sent to comfort us and also to keep us in a divinely informed frame of mind.

First Corinthians 12:7–8 says,

> The manifestation of the Spirit is given to every man to profit withal. For to one is given by the Spirit the word of wisdom; to another the word of knowledge by the same Spirit.

God has provided supernatural means by which we may be inspired to press on to victory in any situation in life. To us the Holy Bible should be God's handbook on life.

God's Word—A Guarantee Unto Itself

As the rain cometh down, and the snow from heaven, and returneth not thither, but watereth the earth, and maketh it bring forth and bud, that it may give seed to the sower, and bread to the eater: So shall my word be that goeth forth out of my mouth: it shall not return unto me void, but it shall accomplish that which I please, and it shall prosper in the thing whereto I sent it.

Isaiah 55:10–11

God declared, "While the earth remaineth, seed-time and harvest, and cold and heat, and summer and winter, and day and night shall not cease" (Gen. 8:22). Essentially God said that as long as the earth remains, there would always be a suitable environment in which His Word will work in the earth as well as in the lives of His people. Our text in Isaiah 55 demonstrates the consistency and surety of God's Word to fulfill the purpose for which it is sent. Our specific activities and assignments all depend upon the principles revealed in these passages.

First, God has given His Word, which sets things in motion. Whatever His specific plans for your life may be, He has committed to furnish you with the necessities needed for accomplishment. Secondly, in this passage the Lord has revealed a type of covenant warranty assuring that His part of the covenant is energized and released to the benefit of any believer who avails himself to it. Further, God has revealed in principle what happens when His Word is received into our hearts as the ground receives the rain and snow that falls from heaven. When received, it causes things to happen. (See also the parable of the sower in Mark 4:2–9.) This is a significant truth to understand how God's Word brings to pass His plans and purposes for our lives, as well as the desires of our hearts.

The Constant Availability of God's Keeping Power

First Corinthians 10:13 states,

> There hath no temptation taken you but such as is common to man: but God is faithful, who will not suffer you to be tempted above that ye are able; but will with the temptation also make a way to escape, that ye may be able to bear it.

This scripture teaches us that God is always available to deliver us from temptation, conditioned by our cooperation. First John 2:16 reveals what I describe as the spheres of human temptation: "All that is in the world, the lust of the flesh, and the lust of the eyes, and the pride of life." The text from 1 Corinthians 10:13 above cites that

God is faithful, meaning that He can always be counted upon to make a way of escape for us.

One might imagine this as an "emergency exit" to deliverance. On the other hand, however, emergency exits in and of themselves do not draw those intended to use them through their openings. Typically printed on or above emergency exits is a sign warning against blocking access to the door. Verses 6–12 in 1 Corinthians 10 list the obstacles that block access to God's provided way of escape:

> Now these things were our examples, to the intent we should not lust after evil things, as they also lusted. Neither be ye idolaters, as were some of them; as it is written, The people sat down to eat and drink, and rose up to play. Neither let us commit fornication, as some of them committed, and fell in one day three and twenty thousand. Neither let us tempt Christ, as some of them also tempted, and were destroyed of serpents. Neither murmur ye, as some of them also murmured, and were destroyed of the destroyer. Now all these things happened unto them for ensamples: and they are written for our admonition, upon whom the ends of the world are come. Wherefore let him that thinketh he standeth take heed lest he fall.

The following is a breakdown of the obstacles mentioned above:

- Lust for evil things (the desire for that which is ungodly)
- Idolatry (the worship of anyone or anything that is not the true and living God)
- Fornication (unlawful sexual relations as well as unlawful spiritual relations)
- Tempting God and Christ (putting God to the test by unbelief, rebellion, provocation, or hardening of the heart)
- Murmuring (complaining)

This list is certainly not exhaustive. In fact it has many derivatives, but we are warned that these things may blind and/or bar our access to the way of escape from temptation.

4

You Say *You* Have Family Problems?

One of the Bible's most remarkable stories of the power of perseverance is the story of Joseph, the son of Jacob. Joseph's story begins in Genesis 37 and continues in chapters 39 through 50.

Jacob made no secret of his preferential love for Joseph. We discover that there is a history of preference in the previous generations as well. Genesis 25:28 reveals that "Isaac loved Esau, because he did eat of his venison: but Rebekah loved Jacob." If we learn nothing else from this verse, it is a perfect example of how much family and parental influence impacts children. Children may not always do as parents say, but they will typically do as parents do.

Satan will stop at nothing to derail the plan that God has for your life, and he will attempt to use "legitimate avenues" to accomplish his diabolical task. *Complex social situations* are among the strategies the enemy uses to achieve his objectives. Complex social situations is the epithet I use to describe hurdles or difficulties in typical domestic relationships. Such hurdles include divorce, children born out of wedlock, single-parent issues, and other perplexing family matters.

Although such situations may be challenging, none is outside of the scope of the Word of God to bring resolution, provided the parties involved cooperate. Proverbs 21:30 states, "There is no wisdom nor understanding nor counsel against the Lord." God is completely immune to evil, and no matter how difficult the personal situation may be, it is always possible with God to realize victory.

Difficulty—particularly with family and loved ones—may pose a daunting hurdle to cross to achieve God's plan and purpose for our lives. It is easy to assign blame for personal digression on antagonizing family members; however, perseverance can overcome even the most sensitive situations.

Joseph's Dysfunctional Family

The following verses outline the severe family problems that Joseph endured on his way to fulfilling God's plan for his life.

> Now Israel loved Joseph more than all his children, because he was the son of his old age:

and he made him a coat of many colours. And when his brethren saw that their father loved him more than all his brethren, they hated him, and could not speak peaceably unto him.

And Joseph dreamed a dream, and he told it his brethren: and they hated him yet the more.

When they saw him afar off, even before he came near unto them, they conspired against him to slay him. And they said one to another, Behold, this dreamer cometh. Come now therefore, and let us slay him, and cast him into some pit, and we will say, Some evil beast hath devoured him: and we shall see what will become of his dreams.

Genesis 37:3–5,18–20

What dire plans these men had for their brother simply because their father loved him more and God gave him dreams. In their eyes they felt that there was provocation enough to justify killing Joseph, but they should never have given place to such envy and hatred.

Bear in mind that Joseph had received two dreams from the Lord that foretold his future greatness, including the fact that his brothers—the very men determined to destroy him—would eventually bow before him. In the heat of a battle, the situation seldom seems bearable, much less escapable. Yet, with God-given dreams and a coat of many colors, the unthinkable happened for Joseph.

As a pastor I tend to look at people as potential "recruits" in the army of God, future soldiers on assignment. God is a purposeful God who does everything He does according to a pattern, based on a principle of His Kingdom. I truly believe there is a God-given purpose for every person on the face of the earth. I further believe that God by the Holy Spirit undertakes the task of engineering circumstances and situations to bring every soul to a place of engagement with Him.

All believers, though many unwittingly, are involved in this awesome process. In fact, Scripture declares that we are "fellow workmen...with and for God" (1 Cor. 3:9 AMP.) God is in the business of raising up agents for the Kingdom of God who are quite capable of flattening, knocking down, wiping out, and overthrowing hell. The enemy of our souls labors continually to prevent the knowledge of the truth from becoming a working knowledge in our spirits. The reason is, he knows that the more we have revelation of God's Word and act on it, the greater our potential will be to break through life's barriers.

Forgiveness—A Key to Overcoming Dysfunction

It would have been easy for Joseph to rationalize dysfunctional behavior based on the things he experienced in his family. Remarkably, these issues did not become besetting sins in his own life. Joseph was exposed to enough family dysfunction to rationalize anger, bitterness, depression, resentment, and a host of other personality disorders. However, in the face of the atrocities perpetrated against him, he—like the apostle Paul—pressed "toward the mark for the prize of the high calling of God" (Phil. 3:14).

Amazingly, there is no record of Joseph retaliating against his brothers or any of his subsequent overseers. It is evident that forgiveness is an indispensable component of perseverance. The power of forgiveness may bring release from otherwise besetting sins that could potentially short circuit the power of perseverance in our lives.

To illustrate this, think about the warnings that are posted around hazardous materials. The signs are there by law in order to protect us from coming into contact with the dangerous substances. Similarly, the Bible posts warnings around hazards as well—the hazards of sin, unforgiveness, and the works of the flesh. May all of us heed the warning signs "posted" in the Scriptures.

Learn to Recognize God's Special Plan for Your Life

Joseph carried a sense of destiny based on the dreams God gave him. He recognized that God had a special plan for his life, and he counted the journey to the prize as valuable as the prize itself. Joseph also knew that the fact that God gave him two dreams about essentially the same thing indicated that He had firmly established the matter and would bring it to pass. (See Genesis 41:32.)

God's plan for you may or may not be revealed through a dream or a vision, but it is clear throughout Scripture that God desires to be integrally involved in our lives. Remember these words from Jeremiah 29:11, "I know the thoughts that I think toward you, saith the Lord, thoughts of peace, and not of evil, to give you an expected end." It is apparent that God does not desire for us to live in uncertainty and fear. On the contrary, when we are filled with God's Word, we become filled with a confident expectation of good. This expectation could be considered to be the lubricant of the machinery of perseverance. A more biblically appropriate term for this confident expectation is *faith*.

Family Issues in the Life of Moses

Admittedly, there are some experiences along the path of life that we would opt out of if given the choice. Many of those "options" reveal the strength of our virtues as well as the ignoble remnants of the Adamic nature lingering in our lives. Born-again Christians on their way to glory should make the most of their journey.

Family issues can be most challenging when one decides to pursue the call of God. The family of Moses is a well-known example of this.

> Miriam and Aaron spake against Moses because of the Ethiopian woman whom he had married: for he had married an Ethiopian woman. And they said, Hath the Lord indeed spoken only by Moses? hath he not spoken also by us? And the Lord heard it. (Now the man Moses was very meek, above all the men which were upon the face of the earth.)
>
> And the Lord spake suddenly unto Moses, and unto Aaron, and unto Miriam, Come out ye three unto the tabernacle of the congregation. And they three came out. And the Lord came down in the pillar of the cloud, and stood in the door of the tabernacle, and called Aaron and Miriam: and they both came forth. And he said, Hear now my words: If there be a prophet among you, I the Lord will make myself known unto him in a vision, and will speak unto him in a dream. My servant Moses is not so, who is faithful in all mine house. With him will I speak mouth to mouth, even apparently, and not in dark speeches; and the similitude of the Lord shall he behold: wherefore then were ye not afraid to speak against my

servant Moses? And the anger of the Lord was kindled against them; and he departed.

Numbers 12:1–9

The woman Moses married was an Ethiopian from outside the camp of Israel, although she was a descendant of Abraham. Miriam and Aaron tried to hide behind the cloak of this family situation, but the real issue was their jealousy toward their "little" brother for the high honor that God had bestowed on him. Zipporah was not the issue; Moses' elevated status with God and His people was.

Verse 2 reveals how Miriam and Aaron permitted their familiarity with Moses to breed contempt. No sibling or any other family member knows a person to the depth that God does, and to presume such knowledge is folly in the eyes of God. The fact that God had chosen Moses to serve as the deliverer and leader of Israel may not have met with the approval of Miriam and Aaron, but God's approval is all that counts.

Although all three of these siblings were used significantly by the Lord, Miriam and Aaron knew that up to that time Moses had spent half of his life as a prince in Egypt and the other half as a shepherd of sheep in Midian. Consequently, they rejected God's choice of leader with their disapproval. This is not an uncommon pattern in Scripture as we discovered in the life of Joseph.

Even Jesus Had Family Issues

Even though Jesus was the Son of God, He, too, encountered issues within his natural family.

> He went out from thence, and came into his own country; and his disciples follow him. And when the sabbath day was come, he began to teach in the synagogue: and many hearing him were astonished, saying, From whence hath this man these things? and what wisdom is this which is given unto him, that even such mighty works are wrought by his hands? Is not this the carpenter, the son of Mary, the brother of James, and Joses, and of Juda, and Simon? and are not his sisters here with us? And they were offended at him. But Jesus said unto them, A prophet is not without honour, but in his own country, and among his own kin, and in his own house. And he could there do no mighty work, save that he laid his hands upon a few sick folk, and healed them.
>
> Mark 6:1–5

One can only wonder what great plans of God have been delayed, hindered, and perhaps quenched because of family issues. A word of wisdom to us from these biblical passages is to seek the approval of God only. We all would like the approval of our families regarding God's plans for our lives, but in the end, only God's approval is crucial.

Meek or Weak

Looking back at our text in Numbers 12 about Moses, we see that verse 3 conspicuously reveals what may be another essential ingredient to the power of perseverance:

> (Now the man Moses was very meek, above all men which were upon the face of the earth.)

This verse is a powerful parenthetical footnote. Some have confused the word *meek* with the word *weak*. *Meek* means submissive or humble, whereas *weak* means lack of strength. I believe Christians often miss great "manifestation moments" with God by transposing the meaning of these two words. In our quest to be bold as a lion, we must be careful not to abandon the fruit of meekness and thus undermine God's desire to show Himself strong in our behalf. (See Prov. 28:1, Gal. 5:22–23 and 2 Chron. 16:9.)

It boils down to being led by the Holy Spirit. It is remarkable that Joseph, Moses, and Jesus all experienced opportunities in which they could have exercised righteous indignation against their detractors. Yet in each case, they operated in meekness, yielding judgment to God, persevering in forbearance. These are beautiful examples of the genuine fruit of meekness.

God's Endorsement Is the One That Counts

God testified of Moses' faithfulness and distinction in the prophetic office:

> He said, Hear now my words: If there be a prophet among you, I the Lord will make myself known unto him in a vision, and will speak unto him in a dream. My servant Moses is not so, who is faithful in all mine house. With him will I speak mouth to mouth, even apparently, and not in dark speeches; and the similitude of the Lord shall he behold: wherefore then were ye not afraid to speak against my servant Moses?
>
> vv. 6–8

That is quite an endorsement!

Miriam and Aaron may have harbored feelings of resentment due to the fact that they remained slaves in Egypt while their little brother Moses enjoyed royal privilege in Pharaoh's palace. It is not an uncommon experience in the body of Christ today where sibling rivalries develop over similar issues in the spiritual arena. We see this often with new believers who enthusiastically embrace the things of God and His Word and as a result begin to experience the rich blessings of God. The temptation to entertain jealousy and resentment comes into play when someone who has been a believer for years seems to be getting fewer results.

All of Joseph's brothers (with the exception of Benjamin) were older, but God gave and revealed the dreams of greatness and leadership to Joseph. Similarly in verse 8 above, God challenged Miriam and Aaron in regard to their respect for Moses as God's prophet in contrast to Moses being their brother. I have discovered that before we are anything to anyone, we are the possession of God. He emphatically states His right of possession and His expectation of those He chooses. "Before I formed thee in the belly I knew thee; and before thou camest out of the womb I sanctified thee, and I ordained thee a prophet unto the nations" (Jer. 1:5).

God knows each of us comprehensively. In fact there are probably many things we have yet to discover about ourselves that God already knows. It seems that life is a journey of discovery. The Lord knows all of the landmarks along the way.

Certainly the Holy Spirit will lead us into all truth, including the truth of God's Word and the truth about ourselves. (See John 16:13.) In more cases than we might readily admit, we don't necessarily desire to acknowledge all of the truth about ourselves. Most if not all of us desire to be considered in the most favorable light, but the light of God's Word illuminates the shadows and recesses of our souls, providing opportunities to submit to biblical correction. No matter the difficulty or level of resistance you may face, if you *decide* to persevere and overcome, you will eventually find yourself across the line to victory.

Overcoming Family Resistance

As a believer confronting family resistance, you may ask, "How do I fulfill the will of God for my life in the face of my family's resistance?" I believe a big clue is found in Proverbs 16:7: "When a man's ways please the Lord, he maketh even his enemies to be at peace with him." Now understand that this verse is not saying that your family members are the enemy. Satan is the real enemy, and he will not bypass the opportunity to manipulate *anyone* to perpetrate his insidious work, including members of your own family.

Ephesians 6:12 clearly states,

> We wrestle not against flesh and blood, but against principalities, against powers, against the rulers of the darkness of this world, against spiritual wickedness in high places.

Regardless of the degree of family resistance one may face, there is never a justifiable cause to violate God's Word. The Bible emphatically points out that solutions to such situations are available through God. Consider the following passages and study them closely:

> My brethren, count it all joy when ye fall into divers temptations; Knowing this, that the trying of your faith worketh patience. But let patience have her perfect work, that ye may be perfect and entire, wanting nothing. If any of you lack wisdom, let him ask of God, that giveth to all men liberally, and upbraideth not; and it shall be given him.
>
> James 1:2–5

> Many are the afflictions of the righteous: but the Lord delivereth him out of them all.
>
> Psalm 34:19

These verses reveal powerful assurances of God's willingness and ability to navigate us safely through life's most severe storms—even those storms that arise in our families!

Loving God Most of All

Have you ever been tempted to love God less than your family? Let's look at what Jesus said about the matter.

> If any man come to me, and hate not his father, and mother, and wife, and children, and brethren, and sisters, yea, and his own life also, he cannot be my disciple.
>
> Luke 14:26

It is important to note in Scripture the places where Jesus declared what a person can or cannot do and what a person will or will not do. The former relates to ability and the latter to willingness. Jesus would never provoke us to do evil in any way, as some might misunderstand this verse to mean. Essentially what He was saying is that whoever does not love father, mother, wife, or anyone less than Him cannot be His disciple.

The point is that no person should hold the place of love in your heart that the Lord does. One of the most vivid examples of this can be viewed in Genesis 22 when Abraham offered up his son Isaac to be sacrificed. Perhaps the most profound example of all is the crucifixion of Jesus where God offered His Son as a sacrifice.

We are commanded to love God with *all* our heart, soul, mind, and strength. (See Mark 12:30.) We are to love our neighbors (all others) as ourselves. (See v. 31.) Yes, we are to love ourselves; it is a component that affects all of our human relationships. But the point of what Jesus said was that we must love God above all.

Choose Family Priorities Wisely

As a pastor I have observed parents who allow their children to convince them that attending Bible study is not as important as their school studies or other activities. Parents are tempted to indulge their children's desires for legitimate things at the expense of their relationship with God. The way to really love your child is to love God more and put Him first. Your child will benefit greatly. Occasionally there will be those times when your child has to be absent from the assembled body of believers due to other scheduled activities, but this should be the exception. We should avoid letting them be absent for every personal convenience. The end of such indulgence is spiritually dangerous.

My wife and I feel that our children's exposure to God's Word and His presence is more important than any other knowledge they can acquire or experience they can have. We certainly recognize the place for natural knowledge, but the knowledge of God provides vital ethical integrity, in contrast to secular knowledge, which is often manipulated to compromise biblical values. Sadly, many people will persevere more for other people and other things than for the Lord and the things of God. I trust this will never become your experience.

5

Go for the Hall of Fame of Faith

God keeps His Word. Never allow your opinion to be based on someone else's spiritual experiences (especially negative experiences) or move you to render a judgment against God's Word. Have you have ever conversed with other Christians in the wake of a disappointing experience who said, "I can't understand it. We were standing on and believing such and such a verse, but it didn't happen"? This may be quite forward and perhaps perceived as presumptuous, but we cannot know with airtight accuracy what anyone believes about God's Word. We are only responsible for what we believe, and we must choose to believe that what God said is true.

> God is not a man, that he should lie; neither the son of man, that he should repent: hath he said, and shall he not do it? or hath he spoken, and shall he not make it good?"
>
> Numbers 23:19

My thoughts are not your thoughts, neither are your ways my ways, saith the Lord. For as the heavens are higher than the earth, so are my ways higher than your ways, and my thoughts than your thoughts. For as the rain cometh down, and the snow from heaven, and returneth not thither, but watereth the earth, and maketh it bring forth and bud, that it may give seed to the sower, and bread to the eater: So shall my word be that goeth forth out of my mouth: it shall not return unto me void, but it shall accomplish that which I please, and it shall prosper in the thing whereto I sent it.

Isaiah 55:8–11

Essentially, these verses state that God's Word always comes to pass. The level you develop in applying the Word and attaining results rests solely between you and God. If you are going to persevere to victory, you can't afford to entertain and rationalize others' failures to attain results. Don't allow the severity of any case or set of circumstances move you to write off divine intervention. This is one of the tactics that the enemy uses to undermine faith. Instead, study the examples of those in Scripture who received manifestations from the Lord.

When he was come down from the mountain, great multitudes followed him. And, behold, there came a leper and worshipped him, saying,

Lord, if thou wilt, thou canst make me clean. And Jesus put forth his hand, and touched him, saying, I will; be thou clean. And immediately his leprosy was cleansed. And Jesus saith unto him, See thou tell no man; but go thy way, show thyself to the priest, and offer the gift that Moses commanded, for a testimony unto them.

And when Jesus was entered into Capernaum, there came unto him a centurion, beseeching him, and saying, Lord, my servant lieth at home sick of the palsy, grievously tormented. And Jesus saith unto him, I will come and heal him. The centurion answered and said, Lord, I am not worthy that thou shouldest come under my roof: but speak the word only, and my servant shall be healed.

When Jesus heard it, he marvelled, and said to them that followed, Verily I say unto you, I have not found so great faith, no, not in Israel.

Jesus said unto the centurion, Go thy way; and as thou hast believed, so be it done unto thee. And his servant was healed in the selfsame hour.

Matthew 8:1–8,10,13

It seems that some people count more on the reasons why God might *not* move on their behalf than the reasons that He will. Consider the following passages:

- Peter opened his mouth, and said, Of a truth I perceive that God is no respecter of persons (Acts 10:34).
- For there is no respect of persons with God, (Rom. 2:11).
- If ye have respect to persons, ye commit sin, and are convinced of the law as transgressors (James 2:9).

I don't believe that God would count Himself in the same group as transgressors by favoring one saint over another. What He does for one, He will do for all who believe.

The Hall of Fame of Faith

The Bible invites you to join what I call the "Hall of Fame of Faith." In the world it seems there are many halls of fame featuring those who have distinguished themselves in a variety of disciplines, events, and activities. Some are cited for all-around superlative performance and others for more specific accomplishments.

Whatever the challenges before you may be, you should be encouraged to know that many brethren have persevered to victory, breaking through the barriers of life. Consider the words of the writer of the book of Hebrews:

Since we are surrounded by so great a cloud of witnesses [who have borne testimony to the Truth], let us strip off and throw aside every encumbrance (unnecessary weight) and that sin which so readily (deftly and cleverly) clings to and entangles us, and let us run with patient endurance and steady and active persistence the appointed course of the race that is set before us. Looking away [from all that will distract] to Jesus, Who is the Leader and the Source of our faith [giving the first incentive for our belief] and is also its Finisher [bringing it to maturity and perfection]. He, for the joy [of obtaining the prize] that was set before Him, endured the cross, despising and ignoring the shame, and is now seated at the right hand of the throne of God. Just think of Him Who endured from sinners such grievous opposition and bitter hostility against Himself [reckon up and consider it all in comparison with your trials], so that you may not grow weary or exhausted, losing heart and relaxing and fainting in your minds.

Hebrews 12:1–3 AMP

I quote this lengthy passage to say that you and I may persevere to victory just like all of those listed here. Isaiah 1:19 says, "If ye be willing and obedient, ye shall eat the good of the land." It all boils down to the strength of your "want to." How strong is your desire to accomplish your objectives in life? The measure will manifest itself in the level of your perseverance. This text in Hebrews 12 encourages us to consider Jesus when up against circumstances that appear to be insurmountable.

Jesus' single, focused objective was to redeem us from the curse of the law. And when you consider that the collective sin of the entire human race was laid upon Him, to call His mission a great undertaking is woefully inadequate. You and I may rest assured that the weight of our assignments and callings will not come near that of Jesus, and we can be confident that through Christ we are well equipped for every challenge we face.

Remember what God said to Joshua:

> I will be with thee: I will not fail thee, nor forsake thee. Be strong and of a good courage…. Be thou strong and very courageous….Have not I commanded thee? Be strong and of a good courage; be not afraid, neither be thou dismayed: for the Lord thy God is with thee whithersoever thou goest.
>
> Joshua 1:5-7,9

I truly believe that in the season ahead, we will witness some of the most exciting manifestations of faith heretofore, because God's people take a bold and fearless stand on His Word. Hopefully you will be counted among those courageous saints.

Categories of Faith

In a series of messages I taught our congregation on faith, we examined Hebrews 11 as a text to illustrate the various categories of faith in which the Hall of Famers distinguished themselves.

There are competitions in many areas of life—academics, athletics, and the arts, to name a few. Athletics, for example, is comprised of baseball, basketball, football, hockey, etc. All of these fall under the general heading of athletics, yet each has it's own unique set of rules that sets it apart from the others.

Hebrews 11 identifies people throughout the Bible whose faith saw them through to victory. Although the situations and circumstances varied, faith was an essential ingredient in every case. And as you closely study each case from its original reference in the Old Testament, you will quickly discover that from start to finish, a persevering attitude was also a necessity.

Looking at Hebrews 11, consider the following categories of faith and the individuals honored in each:

Tried Faith	Abraham (vv. 17–19)
Revelation Faith	Isaac (v. 20)
Prophetic Faith	Jacob (v. 21)
Authoritative Faith	Joseph (v. 22)
Fearless Faith	Amram and Jochebed, parents of Moses (v. 23)
Persevering Faith	Moses (vv. 24–28)
Enduring Faith	Israel (v. 29)
Conquering Faith	Joshua (vv. 30)

Review these other exciting categories of faith and those honored:

> What shall I more say? for the time would fail me to tell of Gedeon, and of Barak, and of Samson, and of Jephthae; of David also, and Samuel, and of the prophets: Who through faith subdues kingdoms, wrought righteousness, obtained promises, stopped the mouths of lions, Quenched the violence of fire, escaped the edge of the sword, out of weakness were made strong, waxed valiant in fight, turned to flight the armies of the aliens.
>
> Hebrews 11:32–34

Reviewing and meditating upon this remarkable list of accomplishments is enough to provoke anyone to move forward in fighting the good fight of faith. As you consider these astounding exploits accomplished by the brethren under the

Old Testament dispensation, look closely at verses 39–40 (emphasis mine):

> These all, having obtained a good report through faith, received not the promise: God *having provided some better thing for us,* that they without us should not be made perfect.

All things considered, what the heroes of faith accomplished is staggering to the natural mind. Yet the verse we just read says that God has provided some better thing for us. What is that better thing? Let's look at Hebrews 8:6:

> He [Jesus] is the mediator of a better covenant, which was established upon better promises.

If what God provided the heroes of faith enabled them to do all that they did, think about the possibilities to us who have received "some better thing" from God—a better covenant established on better promises!

Now, I have heard it said—and perhaps you have also—that records are made to be broken. The Lord Jesus Christ weighed in on this matter when He said,

> Verily, verily, I say unto you, He that believeth on me, the works that I do shall he do also; and

greater works than these shall he do; because I go unto my Father.

John 14:12 (emphasis mine)

Think about that—*greater works* than the Lord Jesus Christ did! He also said,

I am come that they might have life, and that they might have it *more abundantly.*

John 10:10 (emphasis mine)

Purpose and persevere to live on that *more* abundant level, doing *greater* works. Settle for nothing less.

In which category will you make the "Hall of Fame of Faith"?

6

Practical Steps to Breaking Through Life's Barriers

Seeing yourself on the victorious side of your objective is a key essential to victory. In order to break through life's barriers, you must continually visualize yourself overcoming any obstacle that stands between you and your goal. Anything that stands between is closer to your goal than you are; therefore, you must affect a change in that arrangement.

God has equipped each of us with an imagination. I call it the workspace of the mind. Our imaginations enable us to look ahead to what our faith can accomplish. Consider the function of *imagination:* The power of the mind to form a mental image or concept of something that is unreal or not present; such power of the mind used creatively.

Stop looking at where you have been, and begin looking at where you can be. It is no wonder that the very first message preached by both John the Baptist and the Lord Jesus Christ was *Repent*, meaning, change your mind. In other words, change your thinking from *I can't* to *I can*. It is critical that you not underestimate this God-given ability.

Upon observing man's determination to construct the tower of Babel, God stated in Genesis 11:6 (emphasis mine),

> The Lord said, Behold, the people is one, and they have all one language; and this they begin to do: and now nothing will be restrained from them, which they have *imagined* to do.

Practically everything we use in our convenience-driven world was a part of someone's imagination before it was ever created. People confronted with resistance relentlessly countered with persever-ance toward a more convenient solution. Only a few years ago, who would have imagined that most of the world communication would be conducted using hand-held wireless devices? But it has become such a way of life that many of us wonder what we ever did without them.

Proverbs 29:18 says, "Where there is no vision, the people perish." You must first have a vision of success before you can fulfill that vision. And Jesus said in Mark 11:24, "What things soever ye desire, when ye pray, believe that ye receive them, and ye shall have them." According to this verse, answered prayer is preceded by desire. Begin to look at things not as they are, but as they can be. Expect something good to happen. Such an expectation can ignite your dream and provide the momentum you need to realize it.

Our text in Genesis 11 reveals a most interesting insight into the vast and immeasurable potential in the soul of man. The combined exercise of the intellect, emotions, and will (the components of the human soul) have accounted for some remarkable accomplishments, often in the face of formidable circumstances.

An Amazing Story of Perseverance

One of the most fascinating stories of perseverance that I have ever heard was featured in a documentary on the Discovery Channel. This extraordinary experience involved a young French woman. She may have been a teenager at the time of the depicted event. Her mother was a scientist doing research in the great Amazon region of South America. While flying in a commercial aircraft over the vast Amazon jungle canopy, the plane suddenly exploded in midair. The young woman, still strapped in her seat and very much alive, regained consciousness to find herself suspended in the dense canopy of trees. The sole survivor, she immediately released her seatbelt and carefully jumped to the ground some five or six feet below, but her adventure had only begun.

For the next few days, without weapons or a compass, she persevered through some of the most dangerous and deadly uncharted areas in the world. She survived by living off of the land and covering herself with the giant leaves of the exotic foliage in the jungle. Enduring the hot, humid environment filled with biting and stinging insects, some of which bore into her skin to implant their young, she trekked on, remembering something her mother taught her in the event she ever became lost in the jungle. The young woman traveled toward the sound of the river. Amazingly, she did reach the river, which had additional dangers lurking in the moving waters.

Wading down the river some significant distance, she caught sight of a small man-made, makeshift canopy where a canoe was aground. With the unrelenting determination that had brought her through the jungle, she pulled herself up onto the riverbank, climbed into the canoe, and passed out.

Upon returning from a mission into a native village, the owner of the canoe discovered the young woman lying unconscious inside. Quickly, he launched the canoe carrying the dazed and devastated stowaway to a ranger station downriver. Upon arrival, arrangements were made to transport the inadvertent adventurer to a hospital for treatment. As one who had returned from the dead, she survived to chronicle her incredible journey.

The spiritual disposition of this young woman was not mentioned in the documentary, nevertheless, the event was described as "miraculous!" Considering her remarkable survival from the aircraft accident and the subsequent trek, there is no doubt that this woman envisioned her goal, persevering her way through the dangerous barriers to safety.

This thrilling illustration of perseverance underscores the observation and exclamation of the psalmist in Psalm 139:14: "I will praise thee; for I am fearfully and wonderfully made." Life will hurl various challenges our way, but be encouraged by what the Bible says in Psalm 34:19: "Many are the afflictions of the righteous: but the Lord delivereth him out of them all." Beyond the labor and discomfort of childbirth lies the joy of parenthood; over dozens of hurdles and past the finish line is the prize. Choose to believe the Word of God and see yourself persevering and breaking through the barriers of life until you win!

Confident Expectation

Sometimes victory is obscured by self-imposed limitations. Some fail to obtain victory because of the fear of failure. President Franklin D. Roosevelt, on the advent of the United States' involvement in World War II, galvanized the national resolve when he declared, "The only thing we have to fear is fear itself." In other words, it was not a matter of whether we *could* defeat the enemy. The main issue was not to succumb to fear and thus cause our own defeat.

As believers we must develop our walk of faith into being a perpetual journey of confident expectation in God and His Word. Instead of living in the spirit, many if not most, Christians have become accustomed to living life in the flesh, relying heavily on the perception of the physical senses. And, of course, this has been at the expense of developing faith. There are two passages of Scripture that strongly underscore the importance that living by faith should have in our *daily* lives. And it is important to note that virtually everything under discussion in this book can only work by faith.

Hebrews 11:6 says,

> Without faith it is impossible to please him:
> for he that cometh to God must believe that he is,
> and that he is a rewarder of them that diligently
> seek him.

This says to me that faith is not an option for the Christian; it is to be an essential part of our daily lives.

The next passage points out the fact that we simply don't have the luxury of squandering time, considering the signs of the times in which we live.

> See then that ye walk circumspectly, not as
> fools, but as wise, redeeming the time, because
> the days are evil.
>
> Ephesians 5:15–16

Developing a sense of urgency is important in order to break through the barriers of life. Now, I *don't* mean a sense of anxiety or of becoming frantic, worried, and such like. What I do mean is an internal, compelling motivation that propels you toward the fulfillment of God's purpose for your life.

Receive the Good News

I continually challenge God's people to avoid living their lives based on the statistics on the world news. For instance, one statistic reports, in a nutshell, that urban-dwelling single parents most likely will raise children who will occupy prison space. But through faith in God, we can defy the statistics! Jesus is not moved by seemingly hopeless circumstances, and He knows how to deal with them. For example, a man with a demon-possessed son approached Jesus for help with his desperate situation. Jesus said to the man, "If thou canst believe, all things are possible to him that believeth" (Mark 9:23). Jesus responded to the father's faith by rebuking the evil spirits and casting them out. (See vv. 24–27.)

You are not alone in your quest to break through the barriers of life. The enemy has his ways of convincing people that they are isolated and forsaken, unwanted and insignificant. The term *illegitimate* is the societal tag placed upon those individuals born out of wedlock. However, the key synonyms for *legitimate* include *authentic, valid,* and *legal.* In the eyes of God, every living person is authentic, valid, and legal. This is by no means an appeal to promote out-of-wedlock births, but rather to point out that God has provided all men with the opportunity to fulfill His original five-fold plan for man. (See Gen. 1:28.)

God has given to every man the gift that keeps on giving. Upon delivering the birth announcement of the Lord Jesus Christ, the angel of the Lord said, "Fear not: for behold, I bring you good tidings of great joy, *which shall be to all people*" (Luke 2:10, emphasis mine). Did you catch that? He said that the good news of great joy was to be to *all* people. Another way of putting it might be to say that the good news is for whomever will receive it. And there is good news about the good news—no man can keep it from you!

Keep Your Eyes on the Unseen and Eternal

In visualizing or seeing yourself on the victorious side of your objective, avoid the temptation to become distracted by known and unknown resistance. The apostle Paul was a man well experienced in dealing with life's barriers. Consider these powerful words of encouragement that he wrote to the believers at Corinth:

> Our light affliction, which is but for a moment, worketh for us a far more exceeding and eternal weight of glory; while we look not at the things which are seen, but at the things which are not seen: for the things which are seen are temporal; but the things which are not seen are eternal.
>
> 2 Corinthians 4:17–18

What might you consider to be an affliction in your life presently? Few can relate to the intense situations Paul faced, yet he considered them to be "light" and lasting "but for a moment." Paul's attitude was akin to a combat pilot relishing every opportunity for an aerial dogfight. What was his secret? Let's examine the above verses more closely.

You might be thinking, *What possible benefit can there be in affliction?* The key to understanding the answer to this question lies in the word *while*. The benefit is the provision of "a far more exceeding and eternal weight of glory," but that benefit is only realized *"while* we look not at the things which are seen, but at the things which are not seen." While looking at the things that are seen— that is, those things which are perceived by our five physical senses—we are not focused on the things which are unseen. The things that are unseen are those things within the realm of the spirit—that is, those things that are *not* perceived by our physical senses. It is through the unseen realm that we access by faith the grace of God and all that He has made available to us as covenant believers.

Count It All Joy

Convenience has become the "coin of the realm" these days. We in the free world have become a very convenience-oriented society. Most of us want everything done fast with no problems. That philosophy in a phrase is "magical thinking."

In a similar fashion to Paul's remarks that we have just examined, we are encouraged by James to consider negative experiences in our lives as opportunities for growth. Note James' counsel:

> My brethren, count it all joy when ye fall into divers temptations; knowing this, that the trying of your faith worketh patience. But let patience have her perfect work, that ye may be perfect and entire, wanting nothing.
>
> James 1:2–4

It stands to reason that if we had a choice between positive and negative experiences, we would typically choose the path of least resistance. However, both kinds of experiences invariably come to all people. It is important to realize that God's purposes are never entirely thwarted by negative circumstances. His attitude remains forever the same, expressed in the most emphatic assurance of who He is: "I am the Lord." This emphatic declaration of identity is literally self-defining. It reminds me that nothing is too hard for the Lord. It should serve as a constant reminder to you as well.

Through his letter to the Thessalonians, the apostle Paul encouraged them to "prove all things; hold fast that which is good" (1 Thess. 5:21). This proving is not necessarily for the purpose of convincing others, but rather to convince ourselves of all that God has made available to us through Christ. Through life's challenges we will make many discoveries about ourselves. Sir Isaac Newton did not create gravity. He simply discovered its existence. It has always existed, since God created the earth.

Just because you do not physically see the help that God has made available to you does not mean that you are helpless. In fact, circumstances sometimes appear hopeless, and the enemy, as a circling vulture, attempts to evoke from your lips a declaration of defeat. Satan wants to coax the self-defeating words *I can't* from your lips to gain a license to kill, steal, and destroy your dreams. I strongly urge you not to speak any words that let the enemy think he's winning. The devil will try to convince you that you can relieve your feelings of anxiety and uncertainty by once and for all saying, "I quit." No matter how many times he suggests that you can't, don't believe him. Of the devil, the Lord Jesus said, "There is no truth in him. When he speaketh a lie, he speaketh of his own: for he is a liar, and the father of it" (John 8:44).

When you are walking in the will of God, the enemy knows that you are standing at the threshold of victory, and he will desperately attempt to convince you that you cannot cross over. In order to persuade you to give up and quit, Satan may set up an array of appeals that look and sound legitimate. Don't listen to him! Instead, obey the Bible: "Submit yourselves therefore to God. Resist the devil, and he will flee from you" (James 4:7).

Open Our Eyes, Lord

Negative circumstances may sometimes obscure our view of victory and the means by which that victory may come. Looking at the things that are seen can be a temporary disadvantage. Consider the account of 2 Kings 6. The king of Syria was perplexed by a number of thwarted ambushes that he had launched against the children of Israel. In a meeting with his servants, the Syrian king voiced his suspicion that there might be a traitor in their camp who had been conveying his plans to the king of Israel. However, his intelligence sources told him about the prophet Elisha and how he had been supernaturally intercepting the Syrian king's strategies and passing them on to the Israeli king.

As a parenthetical comment, it is interesting to note that in spite of the evidence of the supernatural of God, worldly wisdom still tries to explain it away. Outraged that a man of God was compromising his plans, the Syrian king proposed to apprehend him, which in his mind would rid him of his troubles. Since his counsel surmised they would be up against the supernatural of God, the Syrian king sent a great host of troops to surround the city in which the prophet resided. This is a revelation of the flawed wisdom associated with sin and wickedness.

Ignoring the previous failures of his ambushes against the people of God, the Syrian king assumed that the prophet could not or would not anticipate this new strategy Picking up the story in 2 Kings 6:15, the Bible states,

> When the servant of the man of God was risen early, and gone forth, behold, an host compassed the city both with horses and chariots. And his servant said unto him, alas, my master! How shall we do?

In our modern vernacular, the servant said, "What are we going to do now?" Have you ever felt surrounded on all sides and said that? From the natural perspective, the situation appeared hopeless.

It is in such an environment that the enemy will suggest in broad overtures that you give up and throw in the towel. He'd likely say something like, "And by the way, get ready to become my slave because you have run out of options."

While you hold this scenario in your mind, I want to point out another passage of Scripture that reveals the importance of obtaining and maintaining the Word of God in your spirit. "Thy word have I hid in my heart, that I might not sin against thee" (Ps. 119:11). Unbelief is the basis of all sin. The psalmist, in this passage, revealed the preventative measure for an attack of unbelief. No circumstance or situation can ever cancel or render the Word of God null and void.

I recall a report citing that the ingestion of aspirin tablets at the onset of a heart attack would stave off the attack. That's great if you carry a bottle of aspirin around. But even if you had some with you, the aspirin would still have to be taken before any beneficial effects could be realized. Likewise, but a lot more practical, God has provided His Word as the antidote for unbelief. By "ingesting" the Word of God into our hearts and acting on those words, we can stave off an unbelief attack.

Elisha's servant had a typical reaction to seemingly impossible circumstances. He immediately resolved within himself that there was no hope and no help available. The peculiar thing to me when I read this story is that this servant who worked for a man of God like Elisha never conceived that God might intervene. He undoubtedly up to that time had witnessed a number of miraculous events since this situation was preceded by the nineteenth miracle that God performed through Elisha. This peculiar absence of faith exists in too many of God's people today. Thank God for what the man of God knew: "He answered, Fear not: for they that be with us are more than they that be with them" (2 Kings 6:16). God always outnumbers His enemies. Although that may not be readily discerned by our physical senses, it is nevertheless true.

It is interesting to note that in my pastoral experience when dealing with people who present severe personal challenges, the Holy Spirit has on many occasions prompted me to utter very emphatic encouragement based upon of God's Word. It could be something as simple as, "Continue praising God until victory is manifested." Some believers have allowed themselves to be lulled into thinking that such declarations are mere "cure-alls" to alleviate whatever psychological pressure the enemy is bringing to bear.

This kind of thinking is not a product of the fully persuaded, however. Mature believers understand that in addition to acting on a word of encouragement, they must also continue practicing the other fundamentals of faith.

On the other hand, there are believers like the servant who, instead of taking the word of encouragement at face value, want something more specific to substantiate the word from God. The servant—instead of simply believing that there were more with them than were with the enemy, as was told him by Elisha—was looking to the natural realm to substantiate Elisha's claim. Recognizing the servant's spiritual disadvantage, the man of God prayed for him:

> Lord, I pray thee, open his eyes, that he may see. And the Lord opened the eyes of the young man; and he saw: and, behold, the mountain was full of horses and chariots of fire round about Elisha.
>
> 2 Kings 6:17

I believe you will discover the power of perseverance, "while [you] look not at the things which are seen, but at the things which are not seen" (2 Cor. 4:18, substitution mine). God has given you the spiritual capacity to see yourself on the victorious side of any barrier in life you may face. Do you see that light at the end of the tunnel? Then go for it! Remember: David didn't wait for Goliath to come toward him. He ran to meet the giant. He closed the gap between victory and defeat and saw himself on the victorious side of the challenge. You can do that too!

7

Make *the* Decision, Not Just *a* Decision

There are some interesting and useful points that we may draw from the parable of the prodigal son.

> When he came to himself. He said, How many hired servants of my father's have bread enough and to spare, and I perish with hunger! I will arise and go to my father, and will say unto him, Father, I have sinned against heaven, and before thee.
>
> And he arose, and came to his father.
>
> Luke 15:17–18,20

In this parable, Jesus provided us with a view of the turning point for this reckless individual. First, He "came to himself." He realized that he had no business living among the swine. This step is crucial, because until a person comes to grip with the reality of his present condition, he will never begin the process to emerge from it.

Next the prodigal made a decision to do something about his situation, but that was not enough. It wasn't until he actually followed through on that decision that things began to turn around for him. This is a most critical step, because unless you marshal your will to follow through with your decision, you will remain in your present state. Simply making a decision, but not following through with a decisive act is an exercise in futility.

Another self-defeating lifestyle that should be avoided is living in a state of *until*. This type of person living in this condition is always *about to do* something, but is waiting *until* things change. The person who waits for perfect conditions will never get anything done. Waiting for perfect conditions is my definition for *inefficiency*.

Gather as much information as you can to make an informed decision, then make it. Procrastination is a subtle and stealthy thief of accomplishment and fulfillment. It frames the procrastinator who then as a fugitive must attempt to dodge the bloodhounds of yesterday's undone tasks. When challenged by those who would provoke them to good works, their mouths overflow with the worn-out expression, "one of these days." (See Hebrews 10:24.) What they really mean could be interpreted as "none of these days." But eventually, they must settle the accounts.

Get Wisdom, Then Act

Of course, there are those who, when feeling overwhelmed, ask, "What do I do when I don't know what to do?" As usual, God's Word provides the answer. See God's invitation to you in James 1:5:

> If any of you lack wisdom, let him ask of God, that giveth to all men liberally, and upbraideth not; and it shall be given him.

That is as open an invitation as any I have ever seen. This verse should encourage anyone who is uncertain that the Bible provides real help. The wisdom of God still remains one of the greatest untapped resources in the universe in spite of the great invitation of God. It is essential to understand that action is a vital part of the perseverance equation.

In case after case in the Bible where divine wisdom was sought, God provided instruction upon which men could act. Could God's counsel be ignored? Sadly, yes, invariably to the disadvantage of the individual who indulged himself in such folly. Consider the following proverb if you are ever tempted to defer or ignore godly wisdom: "There is no wisdom nor understanding nor counsel against the Lord" (Prov. 21:30). Ignoring God's counsel is synonymous with self-deception.

I recall a situation presented to me by a church member who owned rental properties. One of his tenants struggled over a period of time to make timely rent payments. Eventually the situation deteriorated to the point that no rent was being paid. The landlord wanted to know how to handle the situation in an honorable way. In dilemmas such as this, some believers may inadvertently ignore God's involvement with the transgressors. Upon a closer examination of this particular situation, much in the way of concession and consideration had been granted to the tenant by the landlord, even to the extent of biblical counsel. In some cases it may be as important for God to motivate the transgressor as it is to work through the one who is transgressed against.

In the wake of the situation, the enemy launched a salvo of fiery darts (accusations) into the mind of the landlord to put him under condemnation. Such thoughts bombarding the mind can certainly impede better judgment, which could result in damage to both parties. But God specializes in conflict resolution, a win/win situation where unity is restored—if both sides are willing to give heed to His counsel.

Jesus is the Lamb of God, and He is also the Lion of the tribe of Judah. Seeing that it is impossible for God to deny Himself, both sides of His personality must coexist, or else one would cancel out the other. The point is that God possesses the capacity to comfort as well confront. Both are necessary for redemption. The end of any matter in which godly counsel is decisively applied will be redemptive. It will clearly reveal God's transcendent glory by turning what Satan means for evil to what God means for good.

Sometimes there is discomfort on the journey from where you are to where you really want to be in life. Don't think it strange because you hit a bump or two along the way to victory. I've experienced some rather bumpy rides on aircraft traveling to minister the Gospel, but I never have opted to get off. I have found that it is better to be on a rough ride with God than to go smooth sailing with Satan.

Dialogue with God is indispensable. Talk to God in prayer just like you would talk to a friend. He won't be tripped up by contemporary "slanguage." He knows your heart, and Jesus said, "Your Father knows what you need before you ask Him" (Matt. 6:8 AMP).

Some say, "Well, then, why bother to ask?" Because it is respectful and beneficial, and it shows obedience to God's Word. Paul put it this way: "Be careful for nothing [don't worry about anything]; but in every thing by prayer and supplication with thanksgiving let your requests be made known unto God" (Phil. 4:6, insertion mine).

Every advance in life is preceded by a quality decision backed up by a commitment to action. High achievers are decisive in their thinking and in their actions. As we mentioned earlier, Jesus told us in Mark 11:24 that answered prayer begins with a desire. You must decide exactly what it is that you want and then make definite decisions. Those decisions must then be followed up with specific actions that correspond to the decisions. This will usher your desires into reality.

Indecisiveness creates inconvenience for both the undecided and others in the wake of their indecisiveness. Have you ever pulled up behind an indecisive person at a fast-food drive-thru window? You are ready with your written list of menu choices from each member of your family of four. But the car in front of you has six undecided individuals who want each order separated.

One of the leading causes of the paralysis of indecisiveness is caused by fear of making a mistake, but there is hope for the believer! "God hath not given us the spirit of fear; but of power, and of love, and of a sound mind" (2 Tim. 1:7). Be bold and act as if the Word of God is true. It is! What word from the mouth of God has ever failed? Have you ever considered the catastrophic results if a word from God *did* fail? Jesus said, "It is easier for heaven and earth to pass, than one tittle of the law [Word of God] to fail" (Luke 16:17, insertion mine). Now, ask yourself, are heaven and earth still in place, the places where God spoke them into existence? The fact that you can answer attests that they are. This is just one of many examples that God's Word never fails.

Say to yourself, "If it is to be, it is up to me!" Will you be one of those who looks back on his life and says, "I wish I had done," or one who says, "I'm glad I did"? Hopefully you will choose the latter. Stop holding yourself hostage. Make the decision to act—and then do it!

Hold Fast to Your Confession of Faith

This step is inspired by Hebrews 10:23:

> Let us hold fast the profession of our faith without wavering; (for he is faithful that promised).

The Greek word *homologia* is translated "profession" in this verse and "confession" in other passages of Scripture. In context they mean the same thing: to say the same as.[2] This step is far more than a mere verbal affirmation to hear the sound of ones own voice. There are powerful forces associated with and brought to bear by confession of faith in God's Word.

The Bible opens in Genesis 1 by attesting to the spoken statements of God and the results of His commands. This is one of many reasons why I never tire of reminding God's people of Ephesians 5:1, which we mentioned at the beginning of this book: "Be ye therefore followers of God, as dear children." We discussed that the Greek word translated "followers" is the same word from which the English word *mimic* is derived. In our own natural state of infancy, among the first behaviors we attempt to mimic is speech. God is emphatically encouraging us to act like Him—in this case, speak like He speaks. Our results may not always come with such expediency, but based on the example set by God, we can be sure that nothing is guaranteed to happen if nothing is ever spoken.

The Scriptures teach profoundly on the power of the spoken word. The word *confession* means to say the same as. Our confessions of faith could be illustrated as drafts or checks drawn on the deposits of God's Word in our hearts. Consider what Jesus said:

> Out of the abundance of the heart the mouth speaketh.
>
> Matthew 12:34:

This is most interesting when taking into account the next verse:

> A good man out of the good treasure of the heart *bringeth forth* good things: and an evil man out of the evil treasure *bringeth forth* evil things.
>
> Matthew 12:35 (emphasis mine)

I emphasized the phrase *bringeth forth* to point out that the words of our mouths reveal the true deposits in our hearts, and they certainly affect and impact our environment. This is why it is so important to have a heart filled with the faith of God. Availing ourselves to the Word of God provides opportunities to "pack it in." As I remember one man of God's observation, he said, "You are your mouth." That is simple, but profound.

Faith Speaks

We must also realize that true Bible faith has a voice. Faith that does not speak is faith that is dead on arrival. In Psalm 116:10, the psalmist wrote, "I believed, therefore have I spoken." In 2 Corinthians 4:13, Paul applied these words to the confession of our faith:

> We having the same spirit of faith, according as it is written, I believed, and therefore have I spoken; we also believe, and therefore speak.

Speaking or confessing what God's Word says is the "natural" way in which faith expresses itself. Jesus emphasized the indispensable role that what we say has in relation to our faith getting things done. Notice the number of times the word *say* is used in Mark 11:23 as Jesus reveals how faith works:

> Verily I *say* unto you, That whosoever shall *say* unto this mountain, Be thou removed, and be thou cast into the sea; and shall not doubt in his heart, but shall believe that those things which he *saith* shall come to pass; he shall have whatsoever he *saith*.

Forms of the word *say* are used four times, indicating the certainty that faith expresses itself by speaking.

Just arbitrarily saying something off of the top of our heads will not produce the results of a genuine confession of faith. The words of our mouths must agree with the Word of God. When we close our mouths and cease confessing what the Word of God says, it is as if God's mouth is closed from speaking into our lives.

The powerful truth behind confession is that a speaking spirit brings power to bear on the physical realm. The Bible clearly teaches that faith is a substance. (See Hebrews 11:1.) It is, then, substantial. It is remarkable that our words or confessions based on God's Word are made of this unique substance that has the power to affect every physical entity known to man. When considering what God accomplished through His spoken Word, why would we ever settle for being spiritually silent?

How genuinely powerful is a confession of faith? Look closely at Romans 10:10:

> With the heart man believeth unto righteousness; and with the mouth confession is made unto salvation.

Through the application of this verse, a sinner becomes a saint. One passes from spiritual death to eternal life. If a confession of faith can bring about such an awesome transformation, what other wonders are possible through the confession of our faith in God's promises? Second Corinthians 1:20 says: "All the promises of God in him are yea, and in him Amen." We can rest assured that God will honor His promises that we speak forth in faith. It seems like foolishness to the natural mind to conceive that spoken words or confessions of faith could possess the power to change anything. Yet the Bible teaches us through precept and example how to perform this vital spiritual function.

In Hebrews 3:1, the Lord Jesus Christ is identified as "the Apostle and High Priest of our profession." (Remember that the words *profession* and *confession* mean the same thing in the context presented.) This means that Christ in heaven serves as our advocate and representative in respect to every Bible promise that we confess with our mouths. The scope of Christ's high-priestly ministry on our behalf in heaven is determined by the scope of our confession on earth.

Some believers have been discouraged from making confessions of faith because they fear ridicule and mocking by others from whom they fear losing respect. Ironically, great multitudes of people practice making "confessions of faith" on a natural level all the time, hoping it will change circumstances. Have you ever noticed the cheering spectators at major sporting events? Perhaps you have been among them. The players will tell you they love the verbal participation of fans because it can be a significant element in changing the momentum of a game. What comes out of your mouth affects your circumstances!

Confession Provides for the Future

Jesus, in the parable of the unjust steward, concluded His teaching saying, "The children of this world are in their generation wiser than the children of light" (Luke 16:8). A close examination of the parable clearly shows that the Lord was not commending any unscrupulous behavior on the part of the steward, but rather the foresight of the steward to provide for his future. My point is that making confessions of faith based on God's Word will certainly impact and provide for your future. The world will use and do everything at it's disposal to affect change toward it's own advantage. How much more should we avail ourselves to the awesome spiritual things that God has put at our disposal.

A man's faith never rises above his confession; in fact, his confession typically reveals what is on deposit in his heart. Jesus said, "Out of the abundance of the heart the mouth speaks" (John 12:34). If you listen carefully to people, you can locate the level of their faith. Just like we expect a child to grow up and mature, we can also encourage people to grow up and mature spiritually. There is a significant difference in the way a small child speaks compared to an adult with much more knowledge and experience. The same is true regarding faith. As a believer matures in faith, the confession of his mouth will mature as well, lining up more and more with God's Word.

8

Developing a Lifestyle of Faith

There is an indisputable connection between faith in our hearts and the Word of God in our mouths. A close look at Romans 10:8-10 clearly illustrates this point:

> What saith it? The word is nigh thee, even in thy mouth, and in thy heart: that is, the word of faith, which we preach; that if thou shalt confess with thy mouth thy Lord Jesus, and shalt believe in thine heart that God hath raised him from the dead, thou shalt be saved. For with the heart man believeth unto righteousness; and with the mouth confession is made unto salvation.

There is some significance to sequential order in Scripture. In each of these three verses, Paul talked about the mouth and the heart, but notice verses 8 and 9. Paul talks about the mouth first, then the heart. But in verse 10, he speaks of the heart first, then the mouth. An interesting cycle becomes apparent.

We essentially begin our Christian experience by confessing words with our mouths. When we speak the Word of God, our ears hear what is said. The Bible says, "Faith cometh by hearing, and hearing by the word of God" (Rom. 10:17). Where does the faith "cometh" to? The answer is the heart, or spirit, of man. Our hearts receive the faith that comes from hearing the Word of God.

To illustrate this principle, consider a fish in water. A fish has gills with which it extracts oxygen from the water to live. As long as water passes (or "cometh") through its gills, oxygen goes into the fish's system. I believe that God has made living by faith as natural and easy as breathing. After all, the Bible says, "The just shall live by faith" (Heb. 10:38). As long as we continue to hear the Word of God, faith will continue to come and our hearts will "breathe" the life of God.

Practice Makes Perfect

By confessing the Word of God with our mouths, we hear it with our own ears and consequently receive it into our hearts, producing faith. As we persistently and consistently practice this cycle, the right confession will begin to flow naturally from our mouths. Then, progressively, we will begin to see the results of the Word working in our lives.

One of my past vocations was that of a professional musician. During that time I was required to memorize hundreds of songs, which I accomplished by practicing them over and over and over. A process was involved. The more I practiced, the more familiar I became with the music. As I *continually* practiced a particular song, I would pick up more and more details that I had missed previously. Eventually I would meet my objective and have each song committed to memory. Interestingly, I discovered that because of that *continual* practice, the actual performances required less effort. (Notice I did not say *no* effort.) It became as natural as breathing. Repetition was the key.

Repetition is the key to holding fast your confession of faith as well. There were times, frankly, that I tired of practicing the same songs over and over, but the results were undeniable. Determine not to ever tire of speaking God's Word, no matter how familiar you are with certain verses of the Bible. The Word of God works; it is alive. It does what God said it would do. The enemy will always attempt to divert your attention from the Word, but don't buy it!

Nothing but the Facts

We all have areas of difficulty that we must deal with from time to time. One of those areas is our feelings, or emotions. I mentioned this in an earlier chapter, but it bears repeating here: it is not what happens *to* you that is the issue, but *how you respond* to what happens to you. This scenario highlights the line of separation between faith and feelings. Faith is always based on the Word of God. Our feelings are based on our senses.

I recall a television program that was popular in the fifties and sixties called *Highway Patrol.* Veteran actor Broderick Crawford played the highway patrolman. In his television role, he encountered numerous situations involving traffic, accidents, and crime. In the course of explaining the events that occurred, the various victims would become emotional at times. These emotions led to exaggerations and distortions of what had actually occurred. Crawford's perceptive character would invariably reply, "Just the facts. Nothing but the facts."

How would this patrolman's accident reports have appeared to his supervisor if he had attempted to document the exaggerations and distorted information given on the basis of the victims' feelings? No clear and concise understanding could have been established. The incidents depicted on the show attested to the fact that something had indeed occurred. The job of the highway patrolman was to find out what that was, with the intention of preventing it from happening again. That is, in part, the objective of this book—to deal with the facts of Scripture and nothing but the facts. We can depend on those facts, or promises, and it will produce results. Faith stands upon God's Word. Feelings may vary. Which sounds more reliable to you?

There are few things, if any, that the words of our mouths do not affect. In a phrase, as we said before, you are your mouth. Confession is an important exercise of perseverance.

Do All That You Can Do

Sir Isaac Newton discovered that a body in motion stays in motion. He further concluded that a body at rest stays at rest.

In Luke 15:20, Jesus revealed that the turning point of the prodigal son's life occurred when he arose and went to his father. As we discussed before, some people, when confronted with what appears to be an impossible or troublesome challenge, surrender to the temptation to shut down and do absolutely nothing; but this is dangerous. Christians are a people called to action. Consider the following verses from the Bible:

Genesis 1:28: "God blessed them, and God said unto them, Be fruitful, and multiply, and replenish the earth, and subdue it: and have dominion over the fish of the sea, and over the fowl of the air, and over every living thing that moveth upon the earth."

1 Timothy 6:12: "Fight the good fight of faith, lay hold on eternal life, whereunto thou art also called, and hast professed a good profession before many witnesses."

James 1:22: "Be ye doers of the word, and not hearers only, deceiving your own selves."

An old adage says, "Sitting still and wishing makes no person great. The good Lord sends the fishing, but you must dig the bait." The real secret to moving forward is getting started. Although we look to God to show Himself strong on our behalf, He encourages us to take the initiative based on the facts that He is God, He is faithful, and He knows all things. He knows what will happen when we act as if His Word is true—it will produce the desired results.

As they approached the Red Sea, Moses and the children of Israel found themselves at a dead end with the enemy in hot pursuit. God's response was to tell Moses to stretch his rod over the sea. This action seemed meaningless, if not ridiculous, in light of the circumstances. Yet when Moses acted on God's Word, doing what he could do, the Red Sea congealed on two sides, creating a path on which God's people continued their journey. After they safely crossed to the other side, the waters flowed back together, becoming a watery grave for the enemy.

Ecclesiastes 11:4 provides one of the many profound principles in Scripture: "He that observeth the wind shall not sow; and he that regardeth the clouds shall not reap." In other words, if you wait for conditions to become perfect, you will not get anything done.

No one should be mislead to believe that God requires nothing on our part of the covenant relationship we have with Him. He knows all of the secrets to success, and one of those secrets is that none of them will work unless you do. God did not give us grape juice; he gave us grapes. If you want the juice, you must squeeze the grapes. You will discover sooner or later that the world is pretty much divided into people who do things and people who only talk about doing things. I would strongly encourage you to become a part of the first group. There is far less competition.

Some people attempt to substitute knowledge for action. Knowledge doesn't work; work does. Have you ever warned someone that if they failed to do a certain thing, negative consequences might occur, yet their only response was, "I know"? Some believers are content only to quote or acknowledge the promises of God, but they do little to experience them. Second Corinthians 1:20 says, "All the promises of God in him are yea, and in him Amen." But the promises are only accessible by faith. James 2:17 states, "Faith, if it hath not works, is dead, being alone." Another way of paraphrasing this verse: faith without corresponding actions is dead.

The Bible clearly reveals what God has made available to us, but there are conditions that must be met. The only thing promised by God unconditionally is His love. Whatever the matter may be, God knows the recipe for victory. As we discussed earlier, recipes are typically followed in a methodical order. Don't allow yourself to become overwhelmed by the complexity of a problem. Begin to take the appropriate steps toward the solution.

There is God's part, and there is our part. Rest assured that God has done His part, and He may, in fact, play multiple parts in resolving life's challenges. But you also have a part, which may be sequential to God's part. In other words, before God does something, something may have to be done by you.

Obedience Sets Things Into Motion

This reminds me of when my wife and I were on the Ten Most Wanted list—of the credit bureaus of America, that is. We were not on the list because creditors wanted to give us credit, but rather they wanted to take it away. At the time, we were just getting started in our Christian experience, and we attended a citywide crusade meeting by a nationally renowned evangelist. I vividly remember the point in the service when the offering appeal was made, and I had no intention of giving anything. Frankly, I was in a spiritual wrestling match with the Lord over giving.

In the spirit, He was impressing me to give, but I was arguing back that all I had to my name was the twenty-dollar bill in my pocket. I reasoned that our apartment rent was due as well as an electric bill of equal amount. On that premise I argued that I could not afford to give because of those obligations. The Lord then asked me if the money in my pocket would pay the bills. I told

Him no. He then responded firmly, "Then go give it." There was something about the way God spoke to me that cut through all of my reasoning and doubts. (See Hebrews 4:12.)

We were seated in the balcony. Finally surrendering to the Spirit of God, I slowly made my way down to the platform and lined up behind many enthusiastic and cheerful givers. It was obvious that they knew something that I didn't, so I just smiled a somewhat nervous smile as I approached the fifty-five-gallon plastic trashcan this evangelist was using for an offering receptacle. I reached carefully into my pocket for the twenty and stood arrested as I released it, tracking its trajectory to the bottom of the container, never to be seen by me again.

What I was not immediately aware of was that God had prompted me to move in a sequential order of events that would bring my wife and me out of financial bondage. To make a long story short, with no recognizable possibility of paying the imminent obligations about which I had argued with God, He opened a door through which we were able not only to pay the rent and utility bill, but we had some left over! Now, by no means were we swimming in an abundance of money, but God, working with our obedience, had set something in motion that changed the entire complexion of our financial situation from that day forward.

If You Know What to Do, Do It!

The Holy Spirit then guided us to teaching from the Word of God regarding tithing and giving offerings. We became faithful in these disciplines, entering into a financial covenant with God. Since that time I can testify that God has met all of our needs according to His Word that says, "Now unto him that is able to do exceeding abundantly above all that we ask or think, according to the power *that worketh* in us" (Eph. 3:20, emphasis mine). Make note of the words *that worketh*. You must realize that even though the Spirit of God can lead you to the water of the Word, He can't make you drink. You must act.

Listen to Jesus:

> Give, and it shall be given unto you; good measure, oppressed down, and shaken together, and running over, shall men give into your bosom. For with the same measure that ye mete withal it shall be measured to you again.
>
> Luke 6:38

The principle and its outcome are always true, but it requires action on our part to access and possess the benefits. Cease wasting time making excuses to God about why you can't. His Word says you can! "Jesus said unto him, If thou canst believe, all things are possible to him that believeth" (Mark 9:23).

A doer of the Word of God is a person who commits himself to acts of faith and obedience. God is God 24/7, 365 days a year. The enemy will attempt to hammer you with accusations, guilt, and condemnation. Satan will argue that the reasons you are experiencing resistance and difficulty is because you did something to provoke it. Sure, believers need to be honest enough to admit that we have supplied ourselves with a share of self-inflicted troubles, but we should also be quick to invoke the advocacy of Jesus according to 1 John 1:9 to receive forgiveness and cleansing:

> If we confess our sins, he is faithful and just to forgive us our sins, and to cleanse us from all unrighteousness.

Bad things don't always happen to good people because good people do bad things. Sometimes bad things happen to good people because they are good. That is a thought-provoking matter, which space prevents us for examining in this text.

My point in bringing up this strategy of the enemy, however, is to encourage you to,

> Cast not away therefore your confidence, which hath great recompense of reward. For ye have need of patience, that, after ye have done the will of God, ye might receive the promise.
>
> Hebrews 10:35–36

Whatever it is you may be undertaking, do the will of God. Use the Word of God to get the enemy out of the way, but do the will of God. Satan is the accuser of the brethren and he may accuse you endlessly, but he cannot change the truth of God's Word. (See Rev. 12:10.) That, my friend, is what you must take a strong stand upon. Paul encouraged the Ephesians,

> Take unto you the whole armour of God, that ye may be able to withstand in the evil day, and *having done all*, to stand.
>
> Ephesians 6:13 (emphasis mine)

If you have done all that you can to stand on the truth of God's Word, remain standing there until God gives further instructions. Some situations require the act of standing or holding fast for a time until the next appropriate sequence of events is initiated. The one sure way to know when that time is, is to be led by the Holy Spirit.

Romans 8:14 says, "As many as are led by the Spirit of God, they are the sons of God."

Mary, the mother of Jesus, spoke some of the simplest but most profound instructions given in the Bible. While she and Jesus were attending a wedding feast in Cana of Galilee, the host ran out of wine. Mary told the servants, "Whatsoever [Jesus] saith unto you, do it" (John 2:5).

God is not obligated to do for us what we can do for ourselves. Going back to our experience on the Ten Most Wanted list of credit bureaus, the situation in which we found ourselves looked impossible. It seemed that we existed on the basis of debt. As is the case of many young couples, we felt the credit card lifestyle was the fast lane to the high life. It was indeed a quick trip, but it came to an even quicker halt. Mountains of bills and debt had piled up. And the only reason for that was that we had been piling them on! Some of the terms associated with various creditors seemed endless and gave the impression that we would never get out of debt. Just looking at our credit reports was oppressive.

The Day of Decision

One day—not someday, but one day—we decided that we were going to get out of debt. I just outlined the spiritual encounter I had with God that led to this decision, but I didn't go into the decisive actions we then had to take. The day finally came when we did take decisive action to eliminate our debt—and it wasn't by declaring bankruptcy. We were adamantly against taking that way out. Friend, if debt is an issue with you, I urge you to do all you can do to be led by the Holy Spirit to discover a way around bankruptcy to resolve your financial woes.

You may have experienced what we were experiencing. Many times I said to myself, *Let's just sit and wait for it to go away.* As you know, problems don't just go away. Eventually, they must be addressed. Fear is one of the most notorious perpetrators of what I call "decisive paralysis," a condition in which the subject is afraid to do anything for fear of what *could* happen. But you will never know if that fear is founded until you take action. Think about it; it is silly to fear the unknown. God Your Father knows it all, from beginning to end! And if you will let Him, He will guide you to a positive outcome.

Behind the scenes, the enemy knows about your bold and courageous decision to take the first step toward your deliverance, and he is going to do his level best to persuade you against taking action.

He will suggest that if you start the process, you may end up opening a can of worms you'll regret for years to come. The enemy will major on the problem, but never mention the solution, God's Word. No matter the complexity or perplexity of the matter before you, meditating on the following verses will increase your strength and resolve.

When incredulous to the possibility of bearing a child well after childbearing years, Sarah laughed in the face of God's promise. God's response is recorded in Genesis 18:14: "Is any thing too hard for the Lord? At the time appointed I will return unto thee, according to the time of life, and Sarah shall have a son." We know the end of the story—God kept His Word.

The prophet Jeremiah exclaimed, "Ah Lord God! behold, thou hast made the heaven and the earth by thy great power and stretched out arm, and there is nothing too hard for thee" (Jer.32:17).

You see, all a person has to do to make a bad situation worse is absolutely nothing. If the matter with which you are dealing requires a call to communicate with someone, pray in the Holy Spirit, get the peace and confidence of God, and make the call. Whoever that person is, make the call. That step will help break fear's grip. Then, believe for the best, not the worst. If you swing and miss, that's only strike one. Stay in the batter's box, and you could very well blast a home run out of the park in terms of breaking through your barrier. One thing is certain, if you never step up to the plate, you'll never know what could happen.

God's Weapons Work

There are any number of domestic situations that remain unchanged or are becoming progressively worse because pride and stubbornness are being permitted to impede the necessary action to change the situation. Often one person is willing to work toward resolution and is willing to change, while the other resists. What does one do to resolve such an impasse? Stand immovably on the truth of God's Word. Who or what is stronger than God? God declared that He would show Himself strong on the behalf of those whose hearts are perfect toward Him. (See 2 Chron. 16:9.) Your part is to keep your heart pure and walk in love; then God can go to work on your behalf.

Take another look at Ephesians 6:13: "Take unto you the whole armour of God, that ye may be able to withstand in the evil day, having done all, to stand." The great news is that all of the spiritual weapons of warfare come with a lifetime guarantee.

Notice Ephesians 6:18:

> Praying always with all prayer and supplication in the Spirit, and watching thereunto with all perseverance and supplication for all saints.

I want you to focus on that phrase, "with all perseverance." The Greek word translated "perseverance" is *proskartereo*, meaning to adhere firmly to.[3] I have found that the tools God has provided to the Body of Christ will never wear out. Unfortunately, however, because of frustration, weariness, impatience, and unbelief, some of God's people drop their weapons, mistakenly thinking they are out of ammunition. No! That's not right! Go to the Word, my friend.

Second Corinthians 10:4 says,

> The weapons of our warfare are not carnal, but mighty through God to the pulling down of strong holds.

These weapons are not carnal, meaning fleshly. They don't wane or grow weaker when applied to the battle at hand. From meditating on these passages, I have drawn the conclusion already stated in Hebrews 6:12: "Be not slothful, but followers of them who through faith and patience inherit the promises." If you do your part, eventually you will inherit the promises. So why not do just that?

Don't Let What You Know Slip

Give due diligence to the things of God. "We ought to give the more earnest heed to the things which we have heard, lest at any time we should let them slip" (Heb. 2:1). These are two observations that we should consider in this verse. First, it talks about being sure that we are diligently adhering to the things we have already heard.

I remember as a child in elementary school a select reading program in which my sixth-grade class participated. During reviews with the instructor, several of us wanted to get ahead of the teacher and the rest of the class by reading on further than we were required to. We soon discovered that by rapidly bypassing the heart of the main lesson, we failed to see the significance of foundational aspects of the story. As a result, we could not make proper conclusions or answer the questions given by the instructor.

My point is that we are to firmly adhere to the basic fundamentals of faith and not abandon them for what may be perceived as deeper revelation. The fundamentals of faith are the operating environment for all biblical revelation. Proverbs 4:7 says, "Wisdom is the principle thing; therefore get wisdom: *and with all thy getting* get understanding" (emphasis mine). Clearly we are to get wisdom and understanding, but we mustn't become so anxious for new revelation that we bypass the basic principles of God that we *already* have.

Secondly, remember our acronym from the word "slip"? Slothful Lazy Inactive Passive. It may assist and encourage you to employ the first observation. These traits should serve as a stark reminder of the importance of giving diligence to the things of God in your life.

Go For It!

I believe that there is no counter measure of the enemy that can successfully stand up against the armor of God. However, there is one condition that does threaten to dismantle the armor, and we are the ones to determine whether or not it is employed. That condition is unbelief. Receive and obey the command of the Lord Jesus as He challenged Thomas in one of His post-resurrection appearances, "Be not faithless, but believing" (John 20:27).

Friend, you do not have to adopt the *Que sera sera* (whatever will be will be) philosophy; you don't have to take every little thing that comes your way. Make up your mind to go after your dreams, your goals, and the desires of your heart that are consistent with godliness.

Opportunities are not on a "star search" looking for you. You must pursue opportunity. Another way of looking at this from a faith perspective is for you to do something through which God can empower you to prosper. Among the many wonderful benefits He assured the diligent listener, observer, and doer of His Word is that He would, "bless all the work of thine hand" (Deut. 28:12). Notice the phrase, *the work of thine hand*. That means the work of *your* hand.

Make sure you do all that you can do now so that at the end of your life, you won't look back and see nothing but a graveyard full of markers with *procrastinator* engraved on them. Don't pass up the opportunities that come your way and let them lie buried behind you. In life, you can't simply wait for success; often you will have to make up your mind to move forward before you see it.

I have found nothing more tragic than a person who has decided that he is through learning, growing, and developing. Such a person is making a statement that he is no longer willing to change. And as we've said before, change is one of the only constants in life. In contrast, I feel privileged to pastor some of the most well-preserved and progressive senior saints anywhere. They seem to personify the expression, "forever young." Most have active lives and are participants in our church ministry. In conversing with those who have determined to live life to the fullest, I have found the common denominator to be their willingness to change. If you are through improving, you are just plain through.

The risk of failure seems to shadow the pursuit of success. But if no one ever risked failing, who would ever succeed? Home-run king Hank Aaron certainly struck out on occasion, but who remembers that? If he had never gone to bat because he was afraid he'd strike out, it is certain he never would have even hit the ball.

Finish What You Begin

Don't let your can'ts outnumber your cans. Do all that you can do, and finish what you begin. Although he lost the 1960 presidential election to John F. Kennedy, Richard Nixon went on to become the thirty-seventh president of the United States in

1968. Mr. Nixon said, "A man is not finished when he is defeated, he is finished when he quits." Never give up!

Mark 11:24: "I say unto you, What things so ever ye desire, when ye pray, believe that ye receive them, and ye shall have them." According to Jesus, answered prayer is preceded by desire. When a desire or dream becomes a determination, the limitless reservoir of God's power becomes available to assist us in our quests.

One of the most common traits found in successful people is their habit of subduing the temptation to give up. I use the word *habit* because these individuals consistently decline the enemy's invitations to quit. Getting started is one thing, finishing is another. The power to persevere is the ability to finish what you begin. There are milestones along the way to our goals that warrant some measure of celebration, but don't park there.

Remain Calm

In the field of aviation, the term, *uneventful* describes a flight free of "events." In other words, it is a flight free of complications or emergency situations. On commercial airlines an instructional demonstration about in-flight safety is provided for the passengers. Included in the presentations is the phrase, "in the event." The point is that there are necessary procedures "in the event" certain things transpire. Stuff happens.

A crucial response to any crisis event is to remain calm. And we can do this by calling on the peace of God and turning our back on fear. This means one must summon self-discipline. More importantly, remember that no matter the degree of difficulty, God does not change. The Lord needs no adjustments. We are the ones to make adjustments.

9

Final Words of Encouragement

You will discover that God is the greatest encourager. Upon succeeding Moses, Joshua led the children of Israel into the Promised Land, greatly encouraged by God. Meditate on these powerful words of encouragement from God, and consider them as being spoken to you:

There shall not any man be able to stand before thee all the days of thy life: as I was with Moses, so I will be with thee: I will not fail thee, nor forsake thee. Be strong and of a good courage: for unto this people shalt thou divide for an inheritance the land, which I sware unto their fathers to give them. Only be thou strong and very courageous, that thou mayest observe to do according to all the law, which Moses my servant commanded thee: turn not from it to the right hand or to the left, that thou mayest prosper whithersoever thou goest.

Have not I commanded thee? Be strong and of a good courage; be not afraid, neither be thou

dismayed: for the Lord thy God is with thee with-
soever thou goest.

Joshua 1:5–7,9

There are three observations we draw from the Lord's statements to Joshua. First, God gave Joshua an assignment. There is something that God wants each of us to accomplish; we all have a purpose for living. I believe that when we acknowledge God in our lives, He will direct our steps to that plan and reveal it to us. (See Prov. 3:6.)

Second, the Lord indicated that resistance to His plan for our lives is inevitable, but futile. He essentially told us to consider affronts and assaults against His plans as having already been deposed by faith. This does not mean that we have no participatory role in the process of addressing and overcoming such resistance. It is an assurance that perseverance in the face of resistance will ulti-mately yield results.

One of the most cunning snares set before men is the fear of man. Proverbs 29:25 says, "The fear of man bringeth a snare: but whoso putteth his trust in the Lord shall be safe." In no uncertain terms, God told Joshua that he did not need to be afraid of anyone. Persevering toward our goals in life will invariably include interacting with people. People have problems. And when—not if—they become a problem, God has encouraged us not to be intimidated. Yes, people can sometimes be a problem. On the other hand, however, God can use them to be part of the solution to problems.

Third, the Lord emphatically assured Joshua that he would not be alone or forsaken throughout the entire course of his God-given assignment. That is a most assuring fact to know. God wants to be involved with what He has given us to do. I have often found myself conversant with Him in the midst of an assignment, and He talks back. I don't talk to Him in a formal-sounding prayer, but rather conversationally, as one would speak with a partner or coworker. After all, we are "labourers together with God" (1 Cor. 3:9).

After the inspiration and discussion, it's time for action. The apostle Paul encouraged the Ephesians saying, "Finally, my brethren, be strong in the Lord, and in the power of his might" (Eph. 6:10). In other words, Paul told them to be empowered by the power of God and have confidence in His ability to get things done. And, I might add, in the wake of that fact, go for it! No matter how daunting an assignment or goal may appear to our flesh, God provides words of assurance that He will see us through. He expects us to cross the finish line. It is not always about crossing that line first, but it is about crossing.

Pass on the Invitation to Quit

In life, we all receive countless invitations to quit and become discouraged. Decline those invitations and seize upon the real opportunities that those attitudes conceal. Refuse to allow yourself to become discouraged by temporary setbacks. The good news about setbacks is that they only come *to pass*—not to stay. Practically everyone who has ever stood on the platform of victory has overcome various types of adversity. Whatever it takes from the Word of God, determine that you are going to do it and press on until you win.

Often the path to the "Promised Land" requires navigating your way through a wilderness. It is important to recognize that the Bible tells more about *how* something can be done rather than *why* something cannot be done. Be willing to make the necessary adjustments and changes that will foster your success. A determined person can do more with next to nothing than a slack-handed person can do with everything at his disposal. When you pick up the hammer of persistence, you can drive the nails of success. Persistence is not optional to anyone desiring to achieve.

When I think of persistence and perseverance, I recall an aviation event reported some years ago. A 747 commercial airliner that in the course of flying over an area in Asia flew into the path of a great cloud of volcanic ash, which had been spewed miles into the air after a sudden eruption. Oxygen starvation quickly extinguished all four engines. But in spite of the circumstances and the fact that the huge airplane began losing altitude quickly, the pilots relentlessly continued efforts to restart the engines. Finally, they succeeded at an altitude of approximately twelve thousand feet, after falling from about thirty-six thousand feet.

What caused them to break through? They remained focused and committed, two vital components of persistence and perseverance. Hundreds of lives were preserved as a result. That is perseverance at its hallmark. Facing certain destruction, the courageous crew resisted being paralyzed by fear and they soared safely to their destination. These men were determined to finish what they had begun. I believe it reasonable to surmise that most people will not confront such dire predicaments, yet in our own situations the challenges we face are difficult enough.

When our church set out to build from the ground up, the outlook was enthusiastically positive. But scarcely into the beginning of the process, challenges began to confront us. There was a major change of contractor. Then there were legislative initiatives on all construction sites in our state requiring significant capital expenditures. We had to comply and were then faced with the pain of the work grinding to a halt. Then there was the improperly installed infrastructure. These are just a few of the issues we encountered; however, we purposed in our hearts to allow these experiences to make us better rather than bitter, and through perseverance and placing our confidence in God, we finally occupied those facilities.

There were many occasions that it seemed like giving in was the only rational thing to do, but we pressed on time after time through all of the issues and challenges. I can testify to you that God is faithful. Whatever He starts, He will finish, and whatever He orders, He will pay for. By God's grace we began, and by God's grace we finished. Even in the face of seeming impossibilities, persistence— that ever driving, intangible trait—enabled us to press on to victory.

Two More Stories of Refusing to Quit

There are two more illustrations of the power of perseverance being applied that I wish to present. One is from the Bible, and the other is an account in the life of a could-have-been loser. The latter illustration involved a small boy whose mother asked him what he wished to become in life. His answer was to be big and athletic.

His answer posed a serious problem to his father and mother and his grandparents on both sides. They were all of small physical stature. His mother's response was remarkably encouraging, however. She told her son that there might not be anything he could do to become big, but there were many things he could do to become an athlete. For a long time it seemed the boy's mother had mistakenly encouraged him in his dream to excel at sports. The young fellow was clumsy and was always the last chosen among his peers, regardless of the sport. In his first year of high school, his coach questioned his continuing pursuit of the "impossible dream" of becoming an athlete.

For most young men, this would have been the final blow, but the boy to whom the coach was talking was Merlin Olsen, who went on to become an all-American high-school football player. Then after his tenure at Utah State as an all-American defensive player, he went on to play fourteen times in the NFL Pro Bowl.

The Woman Who Refused to Lose Heart

I deliberately saved the Bible story for last. It illustrates an even greater disparity with respect to the likelihood of success and the quality decision to finish what was started. It is the parable of the unjust judge, which Jesus told about a widow seeking justice.

> There was in a city a judge, which feared not God, neither regarded man: And there was a widow in that city; and she came unto him, saying, Avenge me of mine adversary. And he would not for a while: but afterward he said within himself, Though I fear not God, nor regard man; Yet because this widow troubleth me, I will avenge her, lest by her continual coming she weary me.
>
> Luke 18:2–5

During the time of Jesus' earthly ministry, widows were at the bottom of the socioeconomic totem pole, if you will. They were commonly oppressed in society, although prophets rebuked Israel for such practices. Yet in spite of her demographic disadvantage, this woman persisted in making her case to the unjust judge who repeatedly turned her away. Finally he relented.

Why did she succeed in the face of such odds? She realized that she had nothing to lose, so she decided to go for it. Sometimes that kind of attitude needs to be employed to ignite self-motivation and perseverance. God is certainly not an unjust judge, but the enemy tries to fill our minds with lies that God isn't as good or as faithful as He says He is. But He is good and He is faithful. And Jesus gave us this parable to help us: "He spake a parable unto them to this end, that men ought always to pray, and not to faint" (Luke 18:1).

The expression *not to faint* means "not to lose heart." What Jesus said in respect to prayer was for us not to give in to doubt, fear, or unbelief in the interim between the request and the answer. No one is a greater finisher than God, and He will be faithful to bring your answer. Finally, when you have done all that you can do, bathe the matter in prayer, for "the effectual fervent prayer of a righteous man availeth much" (James 5:16).

The Battle Cry of Perseverance

Learn the battle cry of perseverance from a man who learned never to quit, Joshua's fellow spy

Caleb. When fully persuaded that God was faithful who had promised the children of Israel a land flowing with milk and honey, Caleb spoke up in the midst of fearful doubters. "Let us go up at once, and possess it; for we are well able to overcome it" (Num. 13:30).

You may not find great crowds in the fraternity of the persevering, but you will find the reward of God. Evidently, this never-quitting attitude of perseverance caught the attention of the Lord. Numbers 14:24 records God's response to Caleb's positive response: "My servant Caleb, because he had another spirit with him, and hath followed me fully, him will I bring into the land whereinto he went; and his seed shall possess it."

Do such bold declarations of faith combined with a persevering attitude produce results? Consider Caleb's testimony:

> Forty years old was I when Moses the servant of the Lord sent me from Kadeshbarnea to espy out the land; and I brought him word again as it was in mine heart. Nevertheless my brethren that went up with me made the heart of the people melt: but I wholly followed the Lord my God. And Moses sware on that day, saying, Surely the land whereon thy feet have trodden shall be thine inheritance, and thy children's for ever, because

thou hast wholly followed the Lord my God. And now, behold, the Lord hath kept me alive, as he said, these forty and five years, even since the Lord spake this word unto Moses, while the children of Israel wandered in the wilderness: and now, lo, I am this day fourscore and five years old. As yet I am as strong this day as I was in the day that Moses sent me: as my strength was then, even so is my strength now, for war, both to go out, and to come in. Now therefore give me this mountain, whereof the Lord spake in that day; for thou heardest in that day how the Anakims were there, and that the cities were great and fenced: if so be the Lord will be with me, then I shall be able to drive them out, as the Lord said. And Joshua blessed him, and gave unto Caleb the son of Jephunneh Hebron for an inheritance. Hebron therefore became the inheritance of Caleb the son of Jephunneh the Kenezite unto this day, because that he wholly followed the Lord God of Israel.

Joshua 14:7–14

Final Nuggets of Inspiration

The following are encouraging nuggets of revelation that I hope will inspire you as we conclude our text:

- Find a way, not an excuse. If you find an excuse, don't pick it up.

- There is a light at the end of the tunnel. Go on through.
- Above the densest fog, the sun still shines.
- What is yet incomplete in your life? Go on, and finish.
- *Now, get off the sideline, and get in the game!*

Perseverance is having a never-quitting attitude. It is a decision to believe you can when circumstances say otherwise. It is the ability to see God when you see no visible means of assistance. Whatever you do, don't take no for an answer from the enemy. When you say yes to God, the devil will not be able to make a no effective in your life. The human spirit is a remarkable creation of God. Don't allow the potential God placed in yours to be wasted by hopelessness.

Persevering involves wholly following the Lord. Be sure that it is the Lord you are following. Be determined to finish what you start, overcome adversity, and enjoy the fruit of your labor.

May God grant you a compelling perseverance to reach the lost and encourage the found, for today we are closer to the return of Christ than yesterday. Cast your days of defeat and despair overboard, and make up your mind to feed your faith and starve your doubts to death.

ENDNOTES

[1] Merriam-Webster's Collegiate Dictionary, Deluxe Edition, Merriam-Webster, Inc. Springfield, Massachusetts, © 1998

[2] The New Strong's Expanded Dictionary of Bible Words, Thomas Nelson Publishers, Nashville, Tennessee, © 2001

[3] Ibid.

A Prayer for Salvation

Dear God in heaven,

I come to you realizing that I have sinned and come short of Your glory. I am so sorry that I have sinned against You. I repent of all my sin, and I confess with my mouth that Jesus Christ, the Son of the living God, is the Lord of my life. In my heart, I believe that You raised Him from the dead that I might be justified—just as if I had never sinned.

Lord Jesus, come into my heart and live in me now. I believe that I receive eternal life through Jesus Christ, my Lord and Savior, and that I am now made a new creation in Christ. I am born again of the Spirit of God. In Jesus' name.

Amen.

If you prayed this prayer to receive Jesus Christ into your heart, write us for the New Christian Kit at the address provided below. The kit will be mailed to you free of charge.

May God's best continually be yours as you feed your faith and starve your doubts to death.

Mail your request for the New Christian Kit to:
Living in Victory
P.O. Box 490346
Atlanta, GA 30349

ABOUT THE AUTHOR

Dr. Joseph M. Ripley, Sr. is pastor and founder of The Body of Christ Church International, USA, a non-denominational church located in College Park, Georgia. What began in 1983 with fifty people is today nearly seven thousand.

The Body of Christ Church International, USA is a multi-faceted ministry which includes School of Ministry, Prison Ministry, Youth Detention Center Ministry, Success in Life Classes, Healing School, Street Reach, Missions - locally and abroad, the IMPACT Tutorial Program, Partners in Education, and Big Brother/Big Sister just to name a few.

Dr. Ripley is widely regarded as an internationally known author, motivational, and conference speaker, travelling from Hawaii to Central America, to Australia. Dr. Ripley can be seen and heard nationally and internationally on the Living in Victory broadcast via television and radio, teaching believers to "Feed their Faith and Starve their Doubts to Death" !

Dr. Ripley is a graduate of the Valley Forge Military Academy in Wayne, Pennsylvania, after which he attended the University of Georgia where he majored in broadcast journalism and political science. He holds a doctorate degree from the New Covenant International Bible College.

Drs. Ripley (Marjanita) are the proud parents of three children, April, Heather, and Joseph, Jr.

For a product catalog by Dr. Joseph M. Ripley, Sr.

Write:
Living in Victory Ministries
P.O. Box 490346
College Park, Georgia 30349

Please include your testimony or help received from this book when you write. Your prayer requests are welcome.